Speak the English the English Speak

COLIN GREY

Speak the English the English Speak

Volume 1

Copyright © 2017 Colin Grey

ISBN- 9781521908242

Speak the English the English Speak

500+ phrases and expressions
(mostly polite)
the English use in
everyday conversation.

What they mean and
how to use them.

Volume 1

Collected from the conversation of friends and family
by Colin Grey

2017

All royalties from the sale of this book go to the
Aidan Woodcock Charitable Trust which
sponsors young professional musicians and helps
them develop their careers.
Details of this charity and its work are available
on www.maiastra.org.

ABOUT THIS BOOK

This book is for anyone who wants to increase their use in conversation of English idiom and colloquialisms. Whether you are a native English speaker or an overseas resident here, this book will help you expand your vocabulary. I've kept it light-hearted with the occasional limerick or verse where that is appropriate (have a look at "Now and again") as this is often the best way to remember things.

You may be fluent in spoken English and proficient at carrying on a conversation but short of the finer points of conversational English – this book is designed to fill the gaps! It's not just understanding what the English person says but knowing how to reply in kind – to use the expressions he or she would use to keep the conversation flowing.

This is the first of three volumes each of 500+ expressions. That is a measure of the richness and diversity of our language. We pinch from other languages (e.g. "bon mot"), change meanings to suit ourselves, transfer epithets from games to daily life, defy logic when it suits us to do so, and often say one thing when we mean something quite different, usually ironically. We enjoy our language!

The structure of each phrase's paragraph is first to explain the meaning of the expression and, where useful, its origin; then to give an example of its use in conversation; and finally an indication of its suitability. Some expressions which are quite proper in the workplace or with friends in the pub would be out of place in the drawing room. This book will help you avoid the pitfalls!

It doesn't set out to be a reference work - there are plenty of those such as Roget or Brewer's which don't always differentiate between the spoken and written word. This book is solely about spoken English. By using it pro-actively - taking, say, a dozen or so expressions at a time and understanding and memorising them for future use – you will increase your fluency. In this way you will enlarge your vocabulary of the vernacular and speak as the English do with the confidence of knowing that every phrase in this book has been collected from everyday conversation.

While compiling these lists I have become aware how much we English love rhyme and alliteration. For example, the expression "A miss is as good as a mile" relies on alliteration for its effect (you could as easily say "a miss is as good as a yard") while "Sticky wicket" uses rhyme. Both derive from cricket, our national game, and have acquired wider meanings through use outside the game. It is these wider meanings that I've concentrated on and I indicate in the text where an expression relies on rhyme or alliteration for its effect.

I hope you will enjoy this book and find it becomes a friend. If you have comments or suggestions for improvement please email me at colingrey365@gmail.com. I look forward to hearing from you!

Colin Grey
Oxshott, Surrey
2017.

CONTENTS

A

Adam's ale
This is an archaic description of plain water! It is best used when a little pomposity is not out of order. "I'm driving so I'd better stick to Adam's ale!" Polite.

ADC – aide de camp
Aide de camp is a military term for a junior officer who assists a staff officer and so carries a measure of his authority. It is also used in civilian life although "personal assistant" is more usual. "Having had a career in the army he always referred to himself as "ADC to the MD" not as his PA." Polite.

Agree with (food)
Some foods upset the eater's stomach – they do not agree with it. "I love liver but if I have it for supper it doesn't agree with me and I lie awake all night with indigestion." Polite.

All over bar the shouting
At the end of a match the supporters of the winning side will cheer and make a lot of noise. If the scores are far apart the game loses interest and it's all over bar the shouting. The same can be applied in any situation where one side is obviously the winner e.g. an election. "He's got more than half the votes already so it's all over bar the shouting." Polite.

All the rage
Currently fashionable – especially for the ladies – a "must have". "Small handbags are all the rage this year but they're not very practical. I've nowhere to put my spectacles." Polite.

All things to all men
This describes a person who changes his behaviour to satisfy the wishes of everyone he meets. "He would do better to be his own man but he tries to be all things to all men and fails in the process". Polite.

Apple of his eye
We owe a lot to William Tyndale, translator of the Bible into English, almost as much as we owe William Shakespeare. "Keep me as the apple of the eye, hide me under the shadow of thy wings", comes from Psalm 17 v 8 and refers to the pupil at the centre of the eye. "She was not the prettiest of his grandchildren but she was the oldest and the apple of his eye". Polite.

Apple pie order
Everything is exactly where it should be. "After breakfast the boy scouts had to clean out their tents

and leave everything in apple pie order for inspection before they went off on their day's expedition." Polite.

Arm and a leg
This is a colourful way of saying that it cost a lot. "I thought I'd take the kids to the zoo for a treat but the entrance fees alone cost me an arm and a leg." Polite.

Ask for trouble
To put oneself into an unfortunate situation either deliberately or unintentionally. "Behaving like that is asking for trouble." "Going out in this weather without an umbrella is just asking for trouble." Polite.

At a pinch
This means in extreme circumstances – if absolutely necessary. "This is a two-man tent but it will sleep three at a pinch." Polite.

At the drop of a hat
Races can be started by the starter holding his hat up high and then dropping it after "Ready, Steady, GO!" So at the drop of a hat means launching into a routine at any opportunity. "He is in favour of Free Trade and at the drop of a hat will bore you for half an hour." Polite.

At the end of the day
Not time-related but used to signify completion. "We've done all we can to persuade our daughter that he's the right man for her but at the end of the day she has to make up her own mind." Polite.

Away to the races

When people go to the (horse) races they plan to have a good day. So this means getting things properly ordered to achieve success. "If we can solve the problem of the site drainage we're away to the races. The rest of the building work will be easy." Polite.

Away with the fairies

Refers to someone who has lost his sense of reason, possibly suffering from Alzheimer's or dementia. It can also be used to imply that someone has not understood the basic facts of an argument. It is a jocular expression and should only be used between friends as it can be misinterpreted. "Looking back over the past three years I realized that Fred's grasp of reality had slipped so much that in reality he was now away with the fairies." Just about polite.

Axe to grind

Having an axe to grind is metaphorical and means either being dogmatic on a subject or having a grievance. "I shouldn't mention Europe to him. He has an axe to grind on that subject and it'll cost you half an hour." Polite.

B

Back burner
This is an analogy from the kitchen hob meaning to allow a project to carry on slowly but without priority. "He has his own priorities and I am disappointed that my project has been put on the back burner." Polite.

Back of his hand
If you slap someone with your open hand it may hurt but it will hurt more if you use the hard back of your hand. "The child wouldn't stop whining so his father gave him the back of his hand." Polite but not allowed today.

Backhander
This is a polite term for an incentive (or even a bribe). "He couldn't get the Planning Committee to approve his development without offering a councillor a backhander to support him." Polite.

Backs to the wall
When you have your back to the wall there's nowhere to escape to so you have to fight your way out. "The British are at their best when they have their backs to the wall." Polite.

Backside
Backside has only one meaning – the rear end of a person, the bit he or she sits on. Never refer to "the backside of the building." Say "The back of the building." For the person, "backside" is the most polite word after "posterior" which is pompous (some ladies may even refer to 'my sit-upon'). Polite.

Bad blood
This is serious ill feeling especially between families or neighbouring groups. "There had always been bad blood between the Montagues and the Capulets until Romeo's love affair with Juliet. Its tragic end began the reconciliation between the two families." Polite.

Baker's dozen
Traditionally if you bought 12 buns the baker put in an extra one as a thank-you. Hence a baker's dozen is 13. Unfortunately with the arrival of supermarkets the practice has stopped! It is also a convenient and upbeat way of avoiding referring to the number 13 which is unlucky. Polite.

Baptism of fire
Babies are baptized with water in church but a baptism of fire means that the subject has had an Introductory experience that is dramatic and more taxing than usual. "It was her first week in charge of

the ward and there were two patient deaths and five A&E cases were admitted. Truly a baptism of fire!" Polite.

Barking up the wrong tree
Addressing the wrong problem. The dog thinks the cat is up one tree when it's up another one. "He talks with conviction but the real issue is quite different and he's barking up the wrong tree." Polite.

Base over apex
This is a euphemism for falling over disastrously. "I had a new set of heels and one caught in a crack in the pavement. It snapped which has ruined the shoe and I went base over apex into the gutter." Polite.

Bat out of hell (like a)
Bats fly quickly and are associated with witches and superstition which in turn are related to hell. The meaning is to travel excessively fast without considering the consequences. "He drove like a bat out of hell to get us there on time." Polite.

Be a lamb
A lady's expression to persuade a man to do something for her that might be beyond the normal call of duty. "Be a lamb and fetch me my handbag from the bedroom ." Polite.

Bear with a sore head
Bears are dangerous animals and a bear with a sore head even more so. Metaphorically when applied to a colleague or acquaintance it means he's in a bad mood. "I should keep your distance – he's like a bear

with a sore head this morning." Polite.

Beat about the bush
To prevaricate or speak evasively. Always refers to the other person: never about oneself. "I tried to be diplomatic about the accident but he said, 'Stop beating about the bush and just tell me what happened.'" Polite but forceful.

Bed of roses
Roses are usually prickly but often highly scented. A bed of roses is thus assumed to be a pleasant thing. But this is used in the negative to indicate problems. "He works hard but his position is no bed of roses." Polite.

Bee's knees
This is classic meaningless English rhyming slang. If bees have knees they are not known for them but the words rhyme and the meaning is "the very best". "There's no question – this new computer is so fast and has so much memory it's the bee's knees." Polite.

Before now
This means in past times and as a habit or custom. "Before now gentlemen wore a suit and tie to church but that is no longer the case. Not even a tie is obligatory, let alone a suit." Polite.

Before your very eyes
Perform sleight-of-hand that makes something disappear even though you are looking very closely. Also used metaphorically. "When it comes to avoiding tax, that accountant can make profits

disappear before your very eyes." Polite.

Below the belt
In boxing there is a defined area in which punches may be landed: in particular on the solar plexus is OK but not on the stomach below it. The belt is thus the lower boundary and anything below the belt is forbidden. Applies metaphorically to contentious general actions or comments. "I could have mentioned that the candidate had been divorced twice but that would have been below the belt, as in this job he wouldn't be responsible for any female staff." Polite.

Bend his ear
To persuade someone by offering favourable arguments. "If you really need finance for your project you'll have to bend his ear during the budget season." Polite.

Bend over backwards
It's difficult to bend over backwards – our bodies are designed to bend forwards. So bending over backwards means going to great trouble especially to negotiate an agreement. "He bent over backwards to reach an agreement but the other party was adamant and would not budge." Polite.

Best thing since sliced bread
In the 1960s the big chain bakeries introduced sliced loaves. The bread was white and soggy but the public bought it due to the influence of TV advertising. So this applies to a new idea that became, or will become, popular especially if it is of little

consequence. "He thinks cruise control in cars is the best thing since sliced bread." Polite but sometimes used sarcastically.

Beyond a joke

Practical jokes have to be borne stoically but sometimes the consequences are more serious than the perpetrators anticipate. Then they are beyond a joke. The expression has widened its meaning to encompass anything the victim is not comfortable with. "Criticising the institution is in order but criticising individual members in public is beyond a joke." Polite.

Beyond the pale

When Ireland was part of the United Kingdom Dublin was the capital and around it, at some distance, a fence was erected called the Pale to keep out the wild Irish. To go beyond the Pale was potentially dangerous and in time the expression has extended to mean doing something that is beyond the social limits. "He was always one for breaking with convention and his actions were frequently considered to be beyond the pale." Polite.

Bit between the teeth

The bit goes in a horse's mouth above its tongue and behind its teeth so that the reins can pull on the soft part of the mouth. If the horse gets the bit between his teeth the rider loses control. So when someone gets the bit between the teeth he operates in his own way regardless of others' wishes. "Once his budget was increased he got the bit between the teeth and spent it indiscriminately." Polite.

Bit by bit
This implies slow and deliberate progress. "I edged my way forward bit by bit in the dark until I reached the end of the passage but then I couldn't remember whether to turn right or left." Polite.

Bit of a devil
Two meanings: 1) a man who takes social risks especially with women; and 2) difficult but not impossible. "To sound my horn, I had to develop my embouchure; I found my horn was a bit of a devil to play." (Flanders and Swann "Ill Wind" – the French Horn). Polite.

Bite the bullet
Before the days of anaesthesia, when surgical operations were painful beyond measure, patients were given a block of wood (a billet?) to bite on. In the battlefield this became a bullet, so the expression means to accept the pain and get on with it. "I had promised Jane I'd be with her at 3 o'clock and wouldn't be late, so despite the bucketing rain I just had to bite the bullet and step out, knowing I'd be soaked when I arrived." Polite.

Bits and bobs
These are small things that accumulate, especially in a lady's handbag. "I've so many bits and bobs that this bag won't do up. I'll just have to buy a bigger bag." Polite.

Black tie
Today "Black tie" on an invitation indicates a semi-formal dinner or party and ladies may wear short or

long dresses. In time past, when the best people always dressed for dinner, a dinner jacket and black bow-tie was informal evening wear for men with short skirts for the ladies. Formal evening wear – white tie and tails – would be indicated on an invitation with the words "Evening Dress" and ladies then wore long dresses. The old certainties are no more and "We're off to a black tie do - very smart", may be the case or it may just be a family birthday party. Polite.

Blackball
Selected against or not elected e.g. "He was blackballed by two members of the Committee." The origin is that in gentlemen's clubs the approval of a new member depended not only on his proposer and seconder but also on the selection process. Members of the Selection Committee voted by dropping a ball into a locked box. If the voter was in favour he dropped a white ball and if against he dropped a black ball. If there is one black ball when the box is opened the applicant fails – but no-one need know who has blackballed him. Polite.

Bloke
A bloke is a man's man who may be attractive to women more for his masculinity than his charm. "My passenger was a good bloke and got out and pushed the car when I got stuck." Polite.

Blot his copybook
In former times when children practised writing script they did so in a copybook that had lines to help them size the letters. Inevitably using steel nibs they

dropped blots of ink as they scratched away. Today it is used metaphorically. "His record would be exemplary if he hadn't blotted his copybook by his affair with the head's secretary." Polite.

Blow a gasket

Old cars were often unreliable and a common reason was lack of compression in the cylinder. This was caused by a leak in the cylinder's gasket seal which created a strong hissing as the vapour escaped. So to blow a gasket is to be visibly upset. "When the boss was told the bad news he blew a gasket and as usual blamed the messenger." Polite.

Blow hot and cold

To be pleasant on one occasion and aloof the next. "The problem with the Smiths is that they blow hot and cold and you can never be sure if they're pleased to see you. It all depends on the company they're keeping." Polite.

Bob's your uncle

In 1887 Robert (Bob) Cecil, Prime Minister of Britain appointed his nephew Arthur Balfour to a post in government for which many considered him too young – so "Bob's your uncle" became a popular catch word. Balfour went on to succeed his uncle as Prime Minister in 1902. The expression gained currency for any task for which there is a simple solution. "How to tie a reef knot – right over left and under, left over right and under and bob's your uncle." Polite.

Bold as brass
More alliteration! It refers to the brass plate announcing for all to see the office of a company or professional firm but is used more often metaphorically. "There he was, bold as brass, on my doorstep waiting to be invited in." Polite.

Bolt hole
A quiet place to which one can retire and be sure not be disturbed. "When his parents died he kept their house in the country as a bolt hole." Polite.

Bon mot
French for "good word": in English an aphorism or pithy saying. "He was judicious in his use of English but couldn't resist the occasional bon mot." Polite.

Bone dry
This means something is as dry as it can possibly be, whether it is the garden, a garment or a white wine. "I ordered a bone dry Sauvignon Blanc but the sommelier said a Sancerre would go better with the fish." Polite.

Bone up
To learn or revise – to get it into your skull. "You'll have to bone up on architectural terms before you go on his course otherwise you won't understand the half of what he's saying." Polite.

Boot on the other foot
This is a reversal of a previous favourable position, at least metaphorically. "He prided himself on his chess skill and was always keen to give advice but when he

met a Grand Master the boot was on the other foot and he realised he had a lot still to learn." Polite.

Bootleg liquor
Spirits made in an illegal still and often of dubious quality. The adjective has been extended to cover goods imported illegally or "fallen off the back of the lorry", film and music recordings made without licence or unauthorised mining. Origin unknown but could it be that the product tasted as though it had been made in a leather boot? Polite

Bounder
A bounder is a man (never a woman) who behaves outside the rules of society. "He flatters her, gets her pregnant and then disappears. He's just a bounder." Polite.

Brass tacks
Cockney rhyming slang meaning "facts" but it is part of a composite expression "get down to brass tacks" meaning examining the detail. "It looks promising on the surface but getting down to brass tacks, it is less favourable than it looks at first sight." Polite.

Bread and butter letter
This is a short letter written to thank your hostess for hospitality or a meal. "I enjoyed my weekend in the country and mustn't forget to write my aunt a bread and butter letter." Polite.

Bright-eyed and bushy-tailed
The person described is alert and wide-awake! Often used as an introductory remark at the beginning of

the day. "Good morning! I hope you all slept well and are bright-eyed and bushy-tailed because we have a lot to get through today." Polite.

Broad as it's long
When there are two alternatives and either is acceptable then the choice is as broad as it's long. It is a useful expression to avoid disagreement. "Fred supports the first proposal but the second also has its merits. As far as I'm concerned it's as broad as it's long." Polite.

Buck stops here
This was US President Harry Truman's famous expression and the motto sat on his desk in the Oval Office of the White House. It means "Ultimately I am responsible." The buck is a marker passed from one poker player to another to indicate who is the dealer. "Passing the buck" means avoiding responsibility but this means accepting it. Polite.

Bull at a gate
A bull charges at a gate without thinking that he may damage himself as well as the gate. The same applies to someone who acts before he thinks. "Once the problem was explained to him he went at it like a bull at a gate without stopping to think through the consequences." Polite.

Bull in a china shop
It's easy to visualise the damage that a bull would do in a shop full of china ornaments. By extension a person who is unaware or uncaring of others' feelings can do similar emotional damage. "The Club

Secretary was in the wrong but the way the Chairman handled it was like a bull in a china shop and in no time he had upset everybody and the Secretary had more support than the Chairman." Polite.

Bullshit baffles brains
This is Armed Services slang – if everything is in the right place and polished, errors may not be seen. "His slick presentation glossed over a number of major defects: it was a case of bullshit baffles brains." Not quite polite.

Burn the candle at both ends
Filling the day with work or play and then partying late into the night. The implication is that you will die an early death. "I burn my candle at both ends: it will not last the night. But Oh my foes and Ah my friends it gives a pretty light." Polite.

Butterflies in my stomach
This is a girlie expression for apprehensions or worries of the kind that men ignore (perhaps at their peril) and is possibly caused by a drop in the blood supply to the stomach. It is used metaphorically to describe nervous fears of exposure to criticism, inability to communicate or general discomfort. "I had butterflies in my stomach at the thought of having to address such a large gathering without any notes." Polite.

By and large
An expression used to summarise comments or options. "The play's plot was weak and it was saved by good acting. So by and large it was a worthwhile

evening." Polite.

By halves

Doing things by halves means skimping or giving insufficient input or enthusiasm. "They promised to support us but they were only prepared to do things by halves and soon we felt we'd be better off without them." Polite.

C

Call the shots
This means to give instructions or be in charge. Originally a military term for ordering the sequence of firing, it is now used generally to describe the person in charge. "By title she's his secretary but she's the one who calls the shots." Polite.

Cat among the pigeons
Pigeons don't like cats and scatter when they see one. Metaphorically it means to cause social havoc and embarrassment. "When he spoke well of Aunt Agatha and her secret lover that set the cat among the pigeons with the whole family, for whom it was a taboo subject." Polite.

Cat nap
A short sleep to refresh one, often after lunch. Also known as "forty winks." "He can't get started in the

afternoon until he's had his cat nap." Polite.

Catch a crab
A rowing term for not getting the oar right into the water and so potentially scooping up water and drenching the passengers. No extended meaning outside rowing. Polite.

Caught with your pants down
Literally this means caught undressed and so embarrassing but it has lost its original meaning and is a quite acceptable way of describing an unexpected change in personal fortunes. "I had a bad cold and had forgotten I was reading the lesson in church. When the vicar reminded me I was caught with my pants down and hadn't time to find a replacement." Polite.

Chalk and cheese
Alliteration meaning "completely different". The phrase can be used of people or propositions. "He's short and sporty and she's tall and intellectual: they're chalk and cheese." Polite.

Chance his arm
Said to have originated when, to end a dispute, one of the protagonists thrust his arm through an open door to shake the opponent's hand not knowing whether it would be taken or cut off, the expression means to take a risk to achieve a desired end. "I decided to chance my arm in a round of golf with the club champion and just hoped I'd play to my handicap." Polite.

Charge over the odds
A trader or skilled man may charge more because of his expensive location or your presumed wealth. "If you insist on living in Knightsbridge you must expect a plumber to charge over the odds, especially on a Sunday." Polite.

Chew the fat
Gossiping or grumbling about undesirable conditions. "We needed a push to get the car started and there were some lads on the street corner but they were too busy chewing the fat to help us." Polite.

Chicken and egg
The eternal conundrum is which came first? This expression is used to show that one thing depends on another which in turn depends on the first. "Electric cars will never be popular until there are enough charging points but no-one will invest in a charging point until there are enough electric cars to make the investment worthwhile. It's a chicken and egg situation." Polite.

Chip in
To contribute to a general kitty e.g. to pay for drinks at the bar or buy a present. Possibly from golf where the classic 3 par hole is a drive, a chip onto the green (which brings the opponents together) and a putt? "When it was proposed that we should buy him a leaving present we all agreed to chip in a fiver." Polite.

Clean as a whistle
One would expect a whistle to be full of bacteria but

perhaps this refers to the sound it makes which is clear and precise. "Her car was dirty and he spent the morning cleaning it. By lunchtime it was clean as a whistle inside and out." Polite.

Clear the decks
Originally a naval term, this is now used universally to mean tidy up or eliminate unnecessary clutter in preparation for a new start. "Before we start on our new project we must clear the decks on the last one and make sure we've dealt with all outstanding matters." Polite.

Cleft stick
Cardinal John Morton was Henry VII's Chancellor in the late C15 and "Morton's Fork" was a form of specious reasoning he used to raise taxes. If a subject spent a lot he must be wealthy (and so could be taxed) and if he didn't he must be saving (and so could be taxed). Either result was bad for the taxpayer and this put him in a cleft (split) stick. "If he accepts the position he will be posted abroad and have to leave his family and if he doesn't he'll be dismissed so he's in a cleft stick." Polite.

Clip round the ear
In past times the correction of boys was often accompanied by a clip (or smack) round the ear – uncaring of the danger to the recipient's hearing. Today it is used metaphorically. "The tutor disagreed with the essay's conclusions and thought the writer was wasting his time; his sharp rebuke was like a clip round the ear for a promising student." Polite.

Clueless

Clues are what detectives look for but clueless is an adjective applied to someone who is useless and incompetent. "He's completely clueless" is schoolboy language but very critical if used of a grown-up. "As a scientist he's brilliant but when it comes to social life he's completely clueless". Polite.

Coals to Newcastle

Newcastle, in the north-east of England, was a centre of the coal-mining industry in the nineteenth century so taking coals to Newcastle is a stupid and unrewarding act. "Their garden is immaculate and everything is carefully planned. Taking them a small shrub as a present would be coals to Newcastle and would probably embarrass them". Polite.

Cock and bull story

A cock and bull story is demonstrably untrue. "I asked him why he wasn't at work yesterday and he gave me some cock and bull story about his wife being ill and having to look after the children." Polite.

Cockles of the heart

Cockles are shellfish but there the likeness ends. The cockles of your heart are there to be warmed by good news or anything that makes you happy. "It warmed the cockles of his heart to hear that his granddaughter had not only passed with honours but had found her true love and announced her engagement." Polite.

Cold feet

When your feet are cold it is difficult to be enthusiastic about anything! This means to lose interest in or be frightened off a plan or suggestion. "He was keen on the idea until he spoke to Fred who was very downbeat. So he got cold feet and wanted no more to do with it." Polite.

Come across

This has two meanings that are only slightly connected. It can mean to discover or stumble on something. "I had never come across this situation before." Or, in negotiations, it can mean delivering the money or information required: "After much wrangling he came across with the documents we'd asked for." Polite.

Come up to scratch

When a target has to be met and points or votes are counted a scratch mark may be made at the point to be achieved. A golfer with a nil handicap is a scratch player. In the negative, not coming up to scratch means not good enough. "He's a good technician but when it comes to managing people he's not really up to scratch." Polite.

Come-uppance

This means defeat, especially of an arrogant person. "Napoleon made himself emperor of all Europe but he got his come-uppance when he met Wellington at Waterloo." Polite.

Coming out of our ears

Means simply "in abundance." It has nothing to do with ears! "Last year we let some poppies seed themselves in the garden and now we've got poppies coming out of our ears." Polite.

Comes to the crunch

This uses alliteration and rhyme for emphasis. It anticipates a difficult situation and introduces a prediction of how the subject will react. "He's full of advice to others but when it comes to the crunch he usually manages to be elsewhere in case he's given the responsibility." Polite.

Common or garden

Originally a horticultural term meaning not a specialist or cross-bred plant, it is now applied to anything that is ordinary or unspectacular. "He thinks his car is a limousine but it's just a common or garden family saloon." Polite.

Cook the books

Preparing false financial accounts requires cooking the books either by manipulating the original records or by misinterpreting the figures. The expression relies on rhyming words rather than rational meaning. "He was not above cooking the books to present a good picture to the shareholders." Polite.

Cool as a cucumber

While owing something to rhyme and alliteration, this is a true reflection of the main attribute of the cucumber - it is cool. This refers to a person (e.g. 007) who is not upset by adverse circumstances. "There she was on the rostrum cool as a cucumber and she spoke for 20 minutes without any notes." Polite.

Copper-bottomed

Sailing ships with wooden hulls were slowed down by barnacles and other sea bodies that stuck to the

wooden hull. The remedy was to sheath the hull in
copper which worked but was very expensive so done
only on important ships like tea clippers. So the
expression means backed by wealth. "I was not
disposed to lend him money but his father gave me a
copper-bottomed guarantee in writing that he would
repay it if his son didn't." Polite.

Country mile
This is longer than a proper mile (a mile is about 1.6
km). In the country, where signposts are few, if you
ask the way your respondent may not wish to
discourage you especially if you're walking and so may
say, "It's about a mile down the road" when it's
actually more. By derivation, "He won the race by a
country mile" means he won easily. Polite.

Crack of dawn
A more prosaic expression is "at first light" i.e. just
before sunrise. But "crack of dawn" has a more
exciting ring to it "They were up at the crack of dawn
and determined to walk 10km before breakfast."
Polite.

Crack of the whip
Nothing to do with horses or hounds! To be given a
fair crack of the whip means to be treated equally
with others. "We are not asking for special privileges.
All we ask is a fair crack of the whip." Polite.

Cream on the bun
The (unexpected) nice thing that makes a proposition
attractive. "He took me to the seaside for the day but
the cream on the bun was that he bought first class

tickets on the train." Polite.

Crying over spilt milk

Complaining ineffectually when something has gone wrong especially if it is not serious. "The car's got a dent in the wing but there's no point in crying over spilt milk. We just have to put up with it and drive on." Polite.

Cut corners

Cutting corners means shortening the route either literally or, more usually metaphorically, to gain an advantage. "He was not above cutting corners to get an order but his customers were never aware of his deception." Polite.

Cut the mustard

This expression owes more to the rhyme than to practice - how many farmers grow mustard? It means that the subject person is not meeting the required standard. "He may be bright and persuasive but the sales figures show he's not cutting the mustard." Polite.

Cut to the chase

In the early days of Westerns in the cinema the best bit was the chase at the end between the stagecoach and the robbers. If the director felt that the story was dragging he would order to cut to the chase to keep the viewers interested. Today it means to ignore intermediate logic and come to a conclusion. "I could list other points against this proposal but to cut to the chase they all indicate that it is not feasible." Polite.

Cut to the quick
William Tyndale, the translator of the Bible into English, identified two classes of men – the quick (i.e. the living) and the dead. To be cut to the quick is to receive a mortal or near-mortal wound. It is used today to mean badly hurt emotionally. "She was cut to the quick by his thoughtless and unkind remark." Polite.

Cuts both ways
An argument can be dangerous if it can be used either for or against a proposition - it cuts both ways like a two-edged sword. "Asking 'Am I my brother's keeper?' cuts both ways because you then have to ask 'Who is my brother?' and the answer is 'Everyone'. Better to keep quiet!" Polite.

Cuts no ice
When an opponent's argument is untenable it cuts no ice with you. The origin is obscure but may be to do with the fact that you can pass a wire through a block of ice but the ice seals up immediately leaving the block whole. "I can understand your father's prejudice against too much immigration but his arguments cut no ice with me." Polite.

D

Damp squib

A squib is a small firework cracker. If it's damp it doesn't make a bang. So a damp squib is a venture, large or small, that is unsuccessful. "It was supposed to be the highlight of the display but it turned out to be a damp squib." Polite.

Damn with faint praise

If a piece of work deserves praise it can be criticized by offering only moderately favourable comments. This is damning with faint praise which leaves the commentator able to escape challenge while being negative. "This is a modest play and the cast treat it with the modesty it deserves." Polite up to a point.

Dead + adjective or adverb

Dead preceding an adjective emphasises its meaning. Thus "dead ordinary" means very ordinary and "dead slow" means at minimal speed. "I asked her one final question and she gave me exactly the answer I wanted so I said, 'You're dead right' and she got the job." Polite.

Death warmed up
Unaccustomed pale complexion often during or after illness. "He says he's over his bout of 'flu but when I saw him he looked like death warmed up." Polite.

Devil may care
Not worrying about details or outcomes: thus irresponsible. "His devil may care attitude towards the rules of the road resulted in serious injuries when we fell off his motorbike." Polite.

Doctor Fell
Doctor Fell is the subject of a short poem "I do not like thee, Doctor Fell. The reason why – I cannot tell. But this I know and know full well, I do not like thee, Doctor Fell". It describes an unaccountable antagonism against a person or proposal – an instinct that something is wrong. "I can't put my finger on it but I don't trust his judgment – it's a Doctor Fell moment and I can't decide whether it's the man or his idea." Polite.

Dog and bone
This is old-fashioned Cockney rhyming slang for the telephone. "I rang up Perkins but got his secretary who said he was on the dog and bone but as soon as he came off she'd get him to give me a bell." Polite.

Dog tired

When a dog is tired it flops on the ground. Dog tired is not just weary but exhausted. "We climbed Table Mountain after lunch but when we got to the top the cable car wasn't working because of high winds so we had to walk down. By the time we got home we were all dog-tired and ready for bed." Polite.

Dog's breakfast

Traditionally the dog is given the left-overs from last night's supper for his breakfast which can be an unappetising mixture. Metaphorically to make a dog's breakfast of something is to spoil it whether it is a table plan for a meal seating the wrong people next to each other or an illogical sermon in church. "He couldn't get the speakers he wanted for his seminar and the result was a dog's breakfast of ill-thought-out presentations." Polite.

Done on a handshake

If businessmen trust each other they can avoid the legal costs of drawing up a written contract and close a deal by shaking hands on it. The London Stock Exchange's motto is, famously, Verbum Meum Pactum – my word is my bond. "Unfortunately this deal was done on a handshake and they now have differences about what was actually agreed. The legal costs will far exceed the cost of drawing up a contract in the first place." Polite.

Done up to the nines

If a person dresses too smartly he or she is done up to the nines with an implication that they may be overdressed for the occasion. "It was a country wedding but the town cousins were all dressed up to the nines and looked out of place." Polite.

Down to earth

This means basic good sense and practicality. It can be a person or a proposal. "He's a practical chap and all his suggestions are down to earth and workable." Polite.

Drinks like a fish

Fishes don't drink but they "breathe" water as mammals breathe air. This refers to anyone who drinks alcohol to excess. "I tell you he drinks like a fish but he never shows any sign of being drunk." Not really polite!

Drop a line

Before emails there were postcards and it was customary to send one when travelling to say that you had arrived safely. "Abelard said to Heloise, 'Don't forget to drop a line to me please.'" (Cole Porter). Polite.

Ducks in a row

Got things organised. "He's got his ducks in a row" means he's sorted out all his problems. Polite.

Dusty answer

Presumably because dust is swept aside a dusty answer is a firm and uncompromising negative. "I asked him if he'd like to come skiing with us and got a dusty answer. It seems they only ski in Meribel." Polite.

Dyed in the wool

If material is dyed after it is woven the dye doesn't always fully penetrate the fibres of the fabric but if the thread is dyed before weaving it does – it is dyed in the wool. So a person who is dyed in the wool is not going to change their mind under any circumstances. "He's a dyed in the wool Tory so you're wasting your time trying to get him to vote otherwise." Polite.

E

Elbow grease
This is the application of vigour to the task of cleaning or polishing. Young apprentices are traditionally sent down to the store for a tin of elbow grease! "If you want your car to look really smart, no matter which polish you use you'll need to apply plenty of elbow grease." Polite.

End of the world (not the)
There are folk who believe the end of the world will come tomorrow but it never does. So this is usually in the negative meaning it doesn't really matter. "It's not the end of the world if we don't hit our target this month. We're ahead on the year as a whole." Polite.

Err on the side of caution
This is a request not to take unnecessary risks and if there is more than one possibility to take the least

risky one. "She knew he loved mountain climbing but she urged him to err on the side of caution especially when out with Eric who could be foolhardy." Polite.

E-type

The E-type Jaguar was an iconic car in the 1960s. It looked like a torpedo and was driven by Stirling Moss in the Le Mans 24 hour race. "E-type" has become a metaphor for anything fast and luxurious and also the occasional joke. "What is long, round and orange and rises out of the ground at 200 kph? Not a nuclear missile but an E-type carrot." Polite.

Everybody who's anybody

"Anybody", here, means an important (or self-important) person. ("He's not just anybody. He's the mayor.") So it is a collection of important people. "It's Derby Day at Epsom so everybody who's anybody in the racing world will be there." Polite.

Eye teeth

The eye teeth are the canines on either side of the incisors in the mouth. They are used for tearing meat and so are essential for survival. In a wider context it means anything valued highly by the subject. "I drive a Porsche and he has a VW Beetle. He'd give his eye teeth to have a car like mine." Polite.

Eye-opener

If new evidence arrives that changes the concept it opens the eyes to new interpretations. It is an eye-opener. Possibly derived from St Paul's blinding on the road to Damascus and subsequent treatment by Ananias. "He'd never thought of it like that so Jack's presentation was an eye-opener for him." Polite.

F

Face to face
If you are face to face with something, you cannot ignore it - it's there and has to be dealt with. "Coming face to face with an inquisitive elephant the best thing is to lie down, be submissive and hope he doesn't tread on you. Whatever you do, don't run - he can run faster than you can!" Polite.

Falls on deaf ears
If advice falls on deaf ears it is not heeded – the ears are diplomatically deaf. "All my investment advice fell on deaf ears and he proceeded to lose a fortune on the stock market." Polite.

Fast and furious
Relying on alliteration, this implies speed but a lack of control. "The crowd rampaged fast and furious through the streets chanting anti-government

slogans." Polite.

Fat lot of good
This means not achieving much benefit. "He spent a fortune in time and money cultivating the councillors in his town but a fat lot of good it did him. His proposal was rejected outright." Polite.

Fathom out
Ships used to measure the depth of water with a line and lead sinker So to fathom out a tricky question or situation is to probe deeply and think carefully before coming to a conclusion. "We could never understand why they were averse to all shellfish but I fathomed out that he must have had a bad experience in the past with a mussel or oyster." Polite.

Feet first
Two meanings: "They carried him out feet first" - he was a corpse. That's how the coffin is brought into the church and turned around and taken out after the funeral service. Alternatively, "He jumped in feet first" – he got involved without thinking it through or assessing the consequences. Both are polite.

Feet on the ground
To have your feet on the ground means to be competent and sensible. "She may be lacking in experience but she has her feet on the ground and I have confidence in her." Polite.

Fill your boots
In the past, fighting forces' alcohol was rationed to maintain discipline and morale. Delivery was

measured in long leather tubs that looked like riding boots. Hence the call, "Fill your boots" was very welcome and has become an invitation to partake generously of whatever good thing is on offer. "The farmer was very generous and often told us boys to fill our boots with apples from his orchard." Polite.

Finger trouble
This originates from sexual foreplay and the full expression is "Pull your finger out and get on with it" but it has lost this immediate connotation and means, more generally, wasting time, not acting or being indecisive. "The project manager suffers from serious finger trouble and he must wake up if we are to get anything done." Not quite polite.

First and foremost
These words mean much the same but alliteration makes them stronger together: they refer to tasks to be done not the importance of different people. "We have three different problems to solve so first and foremost we must decide who is responsible for each and the number of helpers each will need." Polite.

Finishing touches
Putting the finishing touches on something is making sure everything is in order and complete – it may be a portrait or laying the dinner table. "Mum's not quite ready. She still has to put the finishing touches to her make-up but she'll be down in a minute." Polite.

First blood
In a fencing duel the one who inflicts the first wound has an initial advantage. He may not win the bout but

it helps to be the first to draw blood. "After 15 minutes the home team scored a goal so it was first blood to them. Unfortunately they lost their concentration and didn't win the match." Polite.

Fistful
Generally of (paper) money but can be applied to anything that can be held in a hand. "He must have been hungry because when the peanuts came round he took a fistful and stuffed them in his mouth. Not a pretty sight!" Polite.

Fit for purpose
This means able to do the job it was designed to do. More often used in the negative ("It's not fit for purpose.") to describe an organisation or government department that is unable to achieve its goals. Polite.

Fits where it touches
A garment that is too big only fits where it touches the body and it doesn't show the figure to advantage. By extension the phrase can be applied to other circumstances in which the solution is not the best. Polite.

Flavour of the month
Ice cream sellers promote their product by nominating a flavour of the month. Some people change their loyalties or friendships often and the object may be referred to as the flavour of the month. "Time was when he was flavour of the month but he made some mistakes and the boss has found a new protegé." Polite.

Flea in the ear
It's not a pleasant experience having a flea biting the inside of your ear! But this is verbal, not physical – a reprimand. "The waitress was unduly cheeky and I gave her a flea in her ear as well as deducting the tip." Polite.

Flogging a dead horse
A dead horse will not move no matter how much you whip it and the same applies to a proposition that has been discarded for good reason. "By raising again the possibility of granting the retiring members Honorary Life Membership, Fred must realise he is flogging a dead horse. The idea was voted down in committee last year." Polite.

Fly off the handle
This means to lose one's temper and over-react to unfortunate circumstances. "When he heard that his deputy had resigned he flew off the handle and threw things across the room in his rage." Polite.

Fly-by-night
Debtors who wish to avoid their creditors often leave at night to live elsewhere. This is a fly-by-night. "Originally we decided not to give them additional credit as they seemed to be a fly-by-night operation but now we know them better and have confidence in them." Polite.

For all the world
This means unexpectedly or "if you use your imagination". "Ouro Preto in Brazil where they found gold is renowned for the mountain silhouette that

looks for all the world like a miner's thumb." Polite.

For good measure
Tradesmen when weighing goods will sometimes add an extra piece to tip the scales positively for good measure. The phrase is extended to mean to press home a point or establish credibility. "He first gave me the facts and then for good measure added that his senior was convinced that he was right." Polite.

For the birds
A useless idea that has to be discarded. Perhaps because you put out the scraps for the birds to eat. "It was a good plan once but it's been overtaken by events. Now it's just for the birds." Polite.

For the time being
This means for the present and foreseeable future. "We don't know why this water tastes foul and for the time being I suggest you drink beer instead." Polite.

Force to be reckoned with
A person or group offering opposition is a force to be reckoned with and the implication is that this opposition is strong. "The treasury may be only a small group but they hold the purse strings so they are a force to be reckoned with." Polite.

Forty winks
Taking a short nap is known jocularly as having forty winks. (Winking is closing one eye but not the other so the origin is unknown and inexplicable!). "He usually has forty winks after lunch and if he doesn't

he can be grumpy in the afternoon." Polite.

Fourpenny one
A fourpenny one is a hit or smack, usually to the face or head. "The chap next to me on the tube must have been touching up the young lady next to him. She didn't say anything but she suddenly turned round and gave him a fourpenny one on the ear. He just grinned." Polite.

Fresh as a daisy
Daisies are pretty little flowers and rarely look wilted. "She may be 80 but she woke from her after-lunch nap as fresh as a daisy and insisted on going out for a walk in the park." Polite.

Frighten the horses
Said originally about a woman's dress or large hat that was bright or outrageous and so might upset the carriage horses, it is a way of criticising a proposal that is over-the-top or going too far too fast. "It's an excellent idea but we must be careful how we present it. We don't want to frighten the horses." Polite.

Frog in the throat
Frogs croak - which is the sound you make with a frog in your throat. It is the result of an accumulation of phlegm in the back of the throat caused by a head cold or air pollution. "He apologised for his poor performance saying that he had a frog in his throat brought on by the smog in the city." Polite.

Full of beans
When a child is full of beans he or she is happy and

energetic and unstoppable. Some adults are the same at least some of the time. "He's full of beans this morning – it's because his son has passed all his exams." Polite.

Funny feeling

Alliteration helps to emphasise that intuition is at work! "When I heard that he'd left the office early today I had a funny feeling that there was more to it than we'd been told. So I'm not surprised he's been asked to resign." Polite.

G

Game's not worth the candle
Before gas or electricity, light at night was from candles which were not cheap. So if the game you were about to play was deemed to be rubbish you would say it was not worth burning the candle. Hence the phrase means that the reward is not worth the risk. "I was offered a share in a joint venture in Mexico but when I looked at the figures I decided the game was not worth the candle so I declined." Polite.

Gamesmanship
Defined by the author Stephen Potter as "The art of winning without actually cheating", this refers to ways in which the opposition can be upset by, for example, breaking the rhythm of play, feigning an injury, changing the subject in a conversation or arriving late for a meeting. "Djokovic bounces the ball so many times before he serves. It's partly gamesmanship to

put his opponent off." Polite.

Get a grip
This is a peremptory exhortation to take control of a situation - often spoken in frustration to oneself or jokingly to a colleague. "Get a grip, man, before the whole project falls apart." Not really polite.

Get a rocket
"I'll get a rocket for this" means "I'll get told off by the teacher or the boss." There's a slight implication that I don't care that much. "He was in the wrong so I called him in and gave him a rocket." Polite.

Get it into your head
This is an aggressive way of saying "understand". It might be used by a school teacher to pupils or the boss to staff. "Get it into your head that I am not prepared to tolerate this sort of behaviour." Polite but abrasive.

Get my/your skates on
You move faster on skates than on foot – whether roller skates or ice skates. Metaphorically, if time is short you have to get your skates on to get everything done in time. "I have to be down at the clinic in 10 minutes so I must get my skates on otherwise it will be lunchtime before I'm back at my desk." Polite.

Get the drift
To achieve an understanding of a proposition or group sentiment. "If you read this article you'll get the drift of what he means and why he's saying it." Polite.

Get the hang of

To eventually understand a difficult argument or master a complicated process. "She had demonstrated clearly how to bake the cake but it took me three attempts to get the hang of it." Polite.

Get the sack

In the past when a worker was discharged he had to pack up his tools, often in a bag or sack. Hence it means to lose your job. "I warned him - another mistake like that and I'd have to give him the sack in fairness to the other workers." Polite but slang.

Get to grips with

This comes from wrestling as you can't begin to beat an opponent until you've got a hold on him. "This government has failed to get to grips with its two main problems – creating jobs and lowering the exchange rate to make exports cheaper." Polite.

Get your teeth into

Take up a problem or project with enthusiasm and vigour. "He was unsure whether the proposal interested him but he agreed to do it and when he'd got his teeth into it he became very enthusiastic." Polite.

Get up his nose

An itch in the nose or snuff makes you sneeze and, metaphorically, so do unwelcome ideas or opinions. "Something I said got up his nose. It might have been my criticism of his wife's spending habits, but whatever it was he was not pleased." Polite.

Gift of the gab
The ability to talk fluently and persuasively. "It is a prime requirement of a good salesman that he has the gift of the gab. It puts the customer at ease and can save having to answer awkward questions." Polite.

Gin and Jag
The Jag is a Jaguar car – in its day the symbol of executive success – and the gin is gin and tonic. Together they are indicative of affluence rather than wealth and often refer to a district that has estates of executive homes – the gin and Jag belt. "They live in an area that used to be farmland but is now a gin and Jag belt." Polite.

Give a fig
If you don't give a fig for something you don't care for it or what happens to it. "He used to be so interested in what I had to say but now I feel he doesn't give a fig for my opinions." Polite.

Go against the grain
To get a smooth surface wood has to be planed along the grain of the wood. If you plane against the grain you raise up rough patches that are unsightly and unwelcome. By inference it means being contrary or holding opinions that some may find offensive. "I don't trust her and it goes against the grain having to work with her." Polite.

Go nap
Nap is a 5-card trick-taking card game in which each player plays for himself. If you think you can take all the tricks you go nap but you have to declare it

immediately and not wait for your turn in the bidding. By extension it means having the confidence to concentrate all resources on one event or procedure. "They decided to go nap on the new product and it has paid them handsomely." Polite.

Go off the rails
The train runs on rails and we hope it stays on them otherwise there is an accident. So to go off the rails, metaphorically, is to become socially unreliable. "He was fine as long as his wife was with him but when she left him he went off the rails and got drunk too often to be good company." Polite.

Go the extra mile
Means to be prepared to give more help than necessary or expected. "He's always prepared to go the extra mile" means he always gives of his best. A pleasant and complimentary expression – he's a good chap! Polite.

Go to the dogs
Greyhound racing ("the dogs") is not as respectable as horse racing so metaphorically going to the dogs is as low as one can get. By inference it means approaching a state of ruin. "It used to be a fun place for a night out but in recent years it has gone to the dogs." Polite.

Go to the flicks
In the early days of the cinema the black and white picture flickered – hence the name. "How do you fancy going to the flicks tonight? There's a re-run of Caesar and Cleopatra." Polite but old-fashioned.

Goes like the clappers

This is what a young man would say about his motorbike or sports car. There is a connection with bell-ringing: often the ringers speed up at the end of the sequence to hurry you into church. It could also be said of Usain Bolt "He went like the clappers straight out of the starting block." Polite.

Going places

This describes a person who shows signs of future success in his or her career. "She may have changed her job three times in ten years but in each job she's built a platform of experience that has led to a better job. There's no doubt she's going places." Polite.

Good word (put in)

If you put in a good word for someone you give them a favourable introduction or help them to establish their credentials. "She's the new head and if you know her well enough I'd be glad if you'd put in a good word for me." Polite.

Goose pimples/bumps

The English call them goose pimples while the Americans refer to goose bumps. They are a mild and temporary skin rash caused by emotional disturbance which may be embarrassment, the sight of one's lover or even beautiful music. "James Gilchrist's singing was so pure and sincere that it gave me goose pimples." Polite.

Grace and favour

A grace and favour residence is awarded by the monarch to someone (or his widow) who has achieved success in public or national life but may not be financially secure. "General Gale and his wife were granted a grace and favour flat in Hampton Court on his retirement in recognition of his service to his country in two World Wars." Polite.

Grass grow under your feet

If you stand around long enough the grass grows under your feet i.e. you are idle. "He was given a job to do but he let the grass grow under his feet trying to work out the best way of doing it instead of just getting on with it and correcting any mistakes later." Polite.

Great unwashed

Before the days of universal water supplies the lower classes didn't always wash themselves every day. So this is an old-fashioned (and now pejorative) reference to the masses. "As an orator he was better in the House of Commons than addressing the great unwashed." Polite.

Grey matter

The brain is a spongy grey mass so grey matter is the brain and using it. "When he said it was impossible I told him to use his grey matter and work out a solution to the problem." Polite.

Gritted teeth

To accept an instruction unwillingly or agree to a proposition because you have no alternative when you really disagree with it. "He agreed to do as he was asked but added through gritted teeth, 'If you absolutely insist'." Polite.

H

Hackneyed
When an expression is over-used it is said to be hackneyed. Possibly derived from the most common vehicle on the road before the motor car which used to be a "hackney carriage" or taxi. "His books sell well but his prose is full of hackneyed expressions. He is not very original." Polite.

Half a chance
Thanks to the shared vowel half a chance is better than a whole chance! It simply means to be given the opportunity. "Given half a chance and he'll play golf on Saturday morning every weekend." Polite.

Hammer and tongs
The analogy is with a blacksmith who works fast making the shoe to fit the horse's hoof. It can be used in any situation to imply intense vigour, speed and

application. "Once he grasped the urgency of the situation he went about solving it hammer and tongs." Polite.

Hang on to his coat-tails

When someone is doing well if you hang on to his coat-tails you may be carried along as a trusted subordinate. "He never had much in the way of intellect but he hung on to his tutor's coat-tails and look where it got him!" Polite.

Happy as Larry

Whoever Larry is he is evidently very happy – perhaps because his name rhymes with the word? Sometimes used to indicate that the subject is unwell but under medication that blunts his perception. "He was suffering badly but the drugs he's taking have reduced the pain and now he's happy as Larry." Polite.

Hatched, Matched and Dispatched

This is the popular term for Births, Engagements, Marriages and Deaths announcements in the local or national newspapers. "Now that I've reached a certain age I start the paper with Hatched, Matched and Dispatched. Unfortunately it's the last that engages me most." Polite.

Have a decko

An old-fashioned phrase brought back from India by the British army meaning to look at something. It has fallen into disuse since Independence in 1947 but there are still a few older citizens who use it and, of course, it appears in books written before then. "Phew!" said Fred, viewing the cache of jewels, "have a decko at this!" Polite.

Have in mind
Describes an idea or concept not yet fully formed or communicated. "He asked if I enjoyed football so I said, 'What do you have in mind?' as I certainly didn't want to be recruited into a team!" Polite.

Have your cake and eat it
With a piece of cake you have two choices – to eat it or to keep it: you can do one or the other but not both. By analogy this means the subject seeks to get both alternatives in a mutually exclusive situation. "Either Scotland remains part of the United Kingdom and so leaves the European Union or they do not and will have to apply to join Europe. They cannot have their cake and eat it." Polite.

Have your work cut out
This means to be short of the time necessary to complete a task. "There's a lot to do here. You'll have your work cut out to get it all done in time." Polite.

Haven't a clue
Different meanings depending on whether you are talking about yourself or someone else. "I haven't a clue" means "I don't know" as in "I haven't a clue what she means". "He hasn't a clue" – means he is ignorant (see "Clueless" above). Polite about oneself but rather rude about someone else.

Having him on
Innocently deceiving someone. "When I was very young my mother told me that the ice cream van only

played its tune when it had run out of ice cream but she was having me on and I've never forgiven her." Polite.

Head of steam
To get up a gradient a steam train needs all the energy it can muster so the driver waits at the bottom of the hill while the boiler builds up a head of steam. So it means to build up energy and enthusiasm to undertake a project. "We need a big push to finish this job so we must get up a head of steam." Polite.

Head over heels
Falling over completely - so it should really be heels over head! "In his effort to catch the ball he went head over heels into the ditch." Also used to describe teenagers who fall in love. "He's a good-looking boy with good prospects and she's head over heels in love with him." Polite.

Hell-bent
Determined to achieve. "He was hell-bent on getting the order and wasn't above exaggerating the benefits of the product if that would get him his sale." Polite

Hell-for-leather
Going too fast and with determination. The leather is the saddle on a horse but there's no special meaning in the words – just the English love of rhyme. "He always went hell-for-leather down the hill on his bicycle so there was bound to be an accident sooner or later." Polite.

Here today gone tomorrow
This means a worthless operation or venture, one that will not stand the test of time. "We like the owners of the business but their venture is unstable and we fear it is very much here today and gone tomorrow." Polite.

His nibs
His nibs is the most important person around at the moment. It may be the baby or the boss. Boss's secretary to junior manager, "His nibs wants to see you and he's not in a very good mood". Polite up to a point.

Hit into the long grass/Kick into touch
In cricket, if the ball is "lost" in the grass beyond the boundary there is a hiatus while the players search for it and if they do not find it the batting side gains 6 runs. Similarly in football if the ball is kicked into touch playing time is lost. So if a proposal is not acceptable but it would be tactless to oppose it directly a means must be found to delay further discussion. That would be kicking it into touch. Polite.

Hit the nail on the head
To hammer a nail in straight it is essential to hit it squarely on the head otherwise it bends. The same applies to a making a point in discussion or debate. "He hit the nail on the head when he said that for most workers inflation was their biggest worry." Polite.

Hobby horse

A hobby horse is a rocking horse that every child (in the imagination) had in the nursery. Riding it was a satisfying memory that lasted into later life. A person getting on his hobby horse is expounding on a subject on which he has deep-felt feelings. "He started explaining the difference between the two subjects and I realised that this was a hobby horse of his. I was unable to break away for a good 15 minutes." Polite.

Hole in the head

No one likes a hole in the head because if it is a bullet hole it is usually fatal. So this is a jocular expression of dislike. "I'm up to my eyes in work as it is and I need this extra task like a hole in the head." Polite.

Hominem (ad)

A formal term for an argument that attacks the proposer rather than the proposition. That is to say it denigrates the man rather than counters his argument. In politics it has come to mean addressing the particular instance but not solving the underlying problem. "The students' arguments are all ad hominem against the Dean himself and are not related to the policies he is obliged to implement." Polite.

Hook, line and sinker

This comes from fishing. The hook is on the line, the sinker holds the line at the right height above the bottom and the line pulls the fish in. If the fish swallows the bait he's caught and up come hook, line and sinker. Metaphorically it means totally committed to a person or project. "She's a very pretty girl and he fell for her hook, line and sinker." Polite.

Horse's mouth
Straight from the source. Originating in the racing world of tipsters and rumours, it now covers information learned from the originator and not heard second-hand. "What you say is different to what I've heard. Who told you?" "I got it straight from the horse's mouth." Polite.

Horses for courses
Racehorses like some racecourses more than others and the same applies by inference in the world at large. Add in rhyme and you have a classic English expression! "When selling this complex product it is important to send in the right man – it's horses for courses." Polite.

Hot water
Getting into a too-hot bath is painful. Similarly, incurring the displeasure of one's superiors may not be life-threatening but it can be uncomfortable. "Young Fred had no respect for the school's rules and was always getting into hot water." Polite.

House on fire (like a)
Very fast. The timbers in a house are dry and as soon as the fire catches the house goes up in flames. It can be applied to any activity that develops quickly. "I wondered if the public would take to my proposal but once the papers got hold of it, it caught on like a house on fire." Polite.

House room

This does not have to be in a domestic dwelling. You can find house room for an extra filing cabinet in your office or for your neighbour's pets in your shed while they are on holiday. There is a slight implication that it is a temporary arrangement. "I had bought a new car and I asked my neighbour if he had house-room in his drive for the old one until I sold it." Polite.

Hurly-burly

Modern life is one of rushing about to meet deadlines. This is hurly-burly – the speed at which life is lived. Similarly, Mrs Patrick Campbell spoke of "Wedlock: the deep, deep peace of the double bed after the hurly-burly of the chaise-longue" or "After his accident he had difficulty coping with the hurly-burly of city life so he retired to the country where the pace is slower." Polite.

I

If I had my way
The implication of this phrase is that you disagree with what is happening or proposed and can see a better way of doing things. "If I had my way I'd go to Newcastle on the train. It's reliable and much less tiring than driving." Polite.

In a nutshell
Nuts are small so to get something into a nutshell is to reduce it to essentials. "There are arguments for and against but in a nutshell the majority of voters don't want it." Polite.

In a pickle
Pickle comprises onions, cauliflower, cabbage, beans, gherkins and vinegar. It's a mixture of sharp flavours. So someone who is in a pickle is mixed up and can't untangle themselves. "His wife said they really must

go to his uncle's funeral in Newcastle. But he hadn't seen the old man in twenty years and his aunt and cousins are not expecting them so he's in a pickle knowing what to do." Polite.

In good standing

A person who has paid all his debts and has no outstanding complaint against him is in good standing. This is a slightly formal term to define, for example, who may vote in an election or sit on a committee: designed to exclude wayward or awkward members. "I suggested that he might become the president of the tennis club and to avoid showing his embarrassment he said he wasn't sure he was in good standing with the committee." Polite.

In short order

This means briskly and without worrying about hurting peoples' feelings. "When the works manager saw the mess on the factory floor he ordered it to be cleared up in short order." Polite.

In the doghouse

Dogs live in kennels but the "doghouse" is metaphorically reserved for errant husbands or partners who upset their other halves. "I'd love another drink but it will make me late home and then I'll be in the doghouse." Polite.

In the doldrums

The trade winds blow across the Atlantic Ocean from the Caribbean to Europe but sailing north you have to cross the equator before you pick them up. There is an area of flat calm before them and that is the doldrums. By implication it means that you are uncertain what to do or are waiting for someone else's decision. "Until Peter has decided whether he's coming with them they're in the doldrums as to whether to go by car or train." Polite.

In the family way
This is a polite way of saying that a woman is pregnant. "It's sometimes difficult to know whether to stand up for a lady because she's in the family way when she may just be a bit overweight and so feel insulted." Polite.

In the nick of time
Only just in time. "Like the US Seventh Cavalry they arrived in the nick of time so we all set off together." Polite.

In the soup
You don't fall in the soup – you are just in the soup when things go wrong and plans do not work out for you. "He spent all his savings investing in his new design but technology had moved on and he couldn't sell the product so now he's in the soup financially." Polite.

In the sticks
This is the townsman's way of describing the depths of the country – beyond daily contact and social life. "They are artists and they choose to live out in the sticks, well beyond the commuter belt, where they can work in peace." Polite.

In the swim
Being with the crowd, up to date on the gossip, popular and surrounded by friends are all aspects of being in the swim. It has nothing to do with water. "She was pretty and popular until she had her accident. Now she's in a wheelchair she's no longer in the swim." Polite.

In the wars
If a colleague or a child appears with minor wounds or sticking plasters a sympathetic respondent might say, "My! You have been in the wars. How did it happen?" Polite.

In with a shout
In the past in Australia bars shut at 6 pm – very soon after offices closed - so men had to drink fast and the beer was often served through a mobile hose! You had to "shout" your round and if you were heard you might be served and were in with a shout. Needless to say ladies never went into Australian bars! Polite.

In your stride
To take something in your stride means to achieve success without altering any other dispositions. "I gave her this additional responsibility confident that she would take it in her stride and not find the burden too great." Polite.

Infra dig
This is short for the Latin infra dignitatem – beneath one's dignity. It describes an action that falls short of acceptable behaviour. "He was invited to drinks in the house but he went in his sports gear straight after

playing tennis. A bit infra dig really and his hostess wasn't pleased. He should have changed first." Polite.

IOU
An abbreviation of "I owe you" – i.e. an acknowledgement of a debt. "When I had my wallet stolen with all my money and credit cards I had to borrow from the hotel and all I could offer them was an IOU". Polite.

Irons in the fire
The blacksmith can fit more than one shoe at a time so the one he is not shaping is on the coals heating up. By inference a person with many interests has many irons in the fire. "Apart from her career in the Civil Service she was a keen choral singer and an accomplished amateur artist as well as her work for charity. She had many irons in the fire." Polite.

It goes without saying
This is a proposition that is self-explanatory and obvious. "He said that it went without saying that the people vote according to their short-term interest not for what is best for the country in the long term." Polite.

It speaks for itself
When a proposition is self-evident and requires no proof it speaks for itself. "It speaks for itself that the internal combustion engine has been a benefit to mankind despite the pollution it creates." Polite.

It's an ill wind
The full expression is "It's an ill wind that blows

nobody good" but it is so well known that mostly only the first half is used. It means one man's misfortune is another's good fortune. "The heavy rain last week flooded the house but there's a local firm who will clean all the carpets – at a price. It's an ill wind . . " Polite.

J

Jack Spratt
"Jack Spratt could eat no fat: his wife could eat no lean. And so between them when they dined they licked the platter clean." This children's rhyme can be used to suggest that two proposals fit together perfectly. "Your ideas and mine are a perfect match - they fit together like Jack Spratt and his wife." Polite.

Joanna (piano)
This is Cockney rhyming slang and is used today only in a jokey way. The joanna is essentially a pub piano – tinny and probably out of tune - but one on which a popular tune can be played. "He can't read music at all but he can harmonise and you should hear him when he gets going on the old joanna." Polite.

Join the club
Two separate meaning: (1) an expression of

agreement implying that we all know what you are talking about and agree so you are one of the group: (2) getting pregnant. "She went out with him for six months and then discovered she'd joined the club." Polite.

Jump in the lake

A rude way of telling someone that you are not interested in what he is offering or saying. "He tried to get me to invest in his latest venture but I told him to jump in the lake." Rude.

K

Kangaroo court
An informally constituted court with no legal authority but the power to put its decisions into effect. The term is often used to denounce the rulings of the rebel side in an uprising. "Following a show trial in a kangaroo court he was found guilty of treason and executed." Polite.

Keep his nose out of it
The nose is used to sniff things out – not just smells but, metaphorically, situations – so this is a rather aggressive way of telling someone not to interfere. "His colleague was only trying to help but it was a sensitive matter and he told her rudely to keep her nose out of his business." Not really polite.

Keep it under your hat
One possible explanation for this phrase is that

English longbow men kept a spare bowstring under their hat to keep it dry. The meaning is to keep the knowledge in your head and nowhere else. "He told me in confidence about his affair with her and asked me to keep it under my hat." Polite.

Keep the wolf from the door

A snack or light meal to allay hunger. Wolves seek out the weak members of a herd to attack and are thought to enter a forest shack when the owner is too feeble to defend himself. "This isn't a big supper but it will keep the wolf from the door." Polite.

Keep your fingers crossed

For Christians the sign of the Cross wards off evil. Some carry a crucifix for this purpose but in its absence a "cross" can be made by passing the middle finger over the forefinger, (seen sideways on). By extension, this is an exhortation to stave off evil and bring good luck. "The traffic is bad but, fingers crossed, we'll be there on time." Polite.

Keep your hair on

This is an old-fashioned but still well recognised expression asking the hearer to calm down. It is mildly disrespectful. "I was very angry at his approach and even more so when he told me to keep my hair on and calm down." Not really polite.

Keep your pecker up

For the English this is an exhortation to keep your spirits up and be cheerful, especially in adverse circumstances. But for Americans it has a totally different and rather rude connotation as "pecker" is a synonym for the penis. "He was a cheerful man and could be relied on to keep his pecker up even when the going got tough." Polite.

Keep your powder dry

In the days of muzzle-loading hand guns it took a long time to re-load the weapon. So it was important not to shoot until the enemy was close enough to hit and also to keep your powder-horn under your jacket to keep the rain off. By analogy it means to be patient in debate or negotiation and pick the right time to bring forward the important argument. Polite.

Kick into touch *see* Hit into the long grass/Kick into touch

Kill two birds with one stone

It is an accurate thrower who can kill one bird with a stone let alone two! This metaphor identifies an opportunity to do two things with little more effort than doing only one. "If you're going to the shops perhaps you could post these letters for me. It will kill two birds with one stone." Polite.

Knee high to a grasshopper

A grasshopper's knees are higher than his body but he is still a very small creature. This is a jokey way of saying "when he was a very small child." "I tell you he's got football in his blood. He's been playing since he was knee high to a grasshopper." Polite.

Knickers in a twist

Boys wear underpants and girls wear knickers but knickers rhymes with twist. If you get them twisted the only thing to do is to take them off and start again. This is used generally to mean that fundamental mistakes have been made. "The problem with paper Sudoku is that you can go a long way before you find you've got your knickers in a twist. Then you have to start all over again." Quite polite.

Knows his onions
A person knowledgeable or experienced in a particular field knows his onions. "When it comes to dinghy sailing he knows his onions." Polite.

Know the ropes
This is a nautical term – anyone who has seen the intricacy of the rigging on a sailing ship will understand the importance of finding the right rope ("sheet" in nautical terms) to set the sail. today it means the person knows how things work in a particular field. "After twenty years in the industry from the shop floor upwards he knows the ropes." Polite.

Kowtow
The Chinese kowtow requires the lesser man to prostrate himself before the greater and to touch his head on the ground. Metaphorically it means to agree with and act on anything the greater says without demur or dispute. It is usually used in the negative. "I know he expects it but there's no way I'm going to kowtow to him." Polite.

Kudos
Kudos is Greek for praise and the meaning in English is the same. If you get kudos for doing something it

means recognition. "She did a good job organising the conference and earned a lot of kudos from it." Polite.

L

Last straw

This was the straw that broke the camel's back. It applies to a situation when the person referred to has been pushed too far and finally collapses or rebels. "He spent a lot of her money which she put up with but when he admitted he was seeing someone else that was the last straw and she broke off the relationship." Polite.

Laying down the law

Pedantically stating the facts as understood by the speaker (but not necessarily correctly). "A year ago last Thursday I was walking in the zoo when I met a man who thought he knew the lot. He was laying down the law about the habits of baboons and the number of quills a porcupine's got . . ." (Flanders and Swann: The Gnu song). Polite.

Lead with the chin
In boxing the fighter protects his chin with one glove because the chin is a vulnerable target while seeking an opening in his opponent's defences with the other glove. To lead with an unprotected chin is a foolish act. By extension it means relying on a weak point in your case that can be refuted easily. "He had a good case but spoiled it by majoring on a tenuous premise that was leading with his chin." Polite.

Leading question
In a court of law a leading question is one in which the witness is guided by counsel to the required answer. This practice is banned since the evidence is then biased. Outside the court-room it has come to mean simply a very important question. This is a wrong use of the term but to challenge it is to be pedantic. "He said the leading question was whether the planning authorities would grant permission for the development. Without this the project was dead." Polite.

Learning curve
Learning curves are usually steep: it means embracing new ideas or procedures that at first are difficult to understand or memorise. "If we buy this new machinery we shall have a steep learning curve until we have mastered all the details of how it operates." Polite.

Leave no stone unturned
This means to be extra-diligent in researching a case. "In his effort to discover the truth he interviewed everybody remotely connected to the crime and left

no stone unturned." Polite.

Let bygones be bygones

Things that have happened in the past are often best left there - that is the meaning of this phrase. "We may have had our differences in the past but now it's time to let bygones be bygones." Polite.

Let on

To let on is to tell a semi-secret to someone either inadvertently or intentionally. "If you have a secret the best way to keep it a secret is not to let on that you have a secret." Polite.

Let the cat out of the bag

To disclose information unintentionally. "She was keeping quiet about her party because she couldn't afford to invite all her friends but one evening she let the cat out of the bag and now it's going to cost her much more than she had budgeted." Polite.

Let the dog see the rabbit

If the dog doesn't see the rabbit it will not chase and catch it. So the message is not to interfere but let a person get on with his or her allotted task. "He was impatient speed up the project but I advised him to let the dog see the rabbit as I had faith in the selected team that they would succeed." Polite.

Let your hair down

In the days when ladies put their hair up, letting it down implied relaxing. It has taken on a stronger meaning now and means speaking your mind and ignoring tact or persuasion. "After some provocation he let his hair down and told the meeting exactly what he thought." Polite.

Lib (ad)
Abbreviation of Latin ad libitum = to one's own pleasure or improvising. Used exclusively about speaking – not having or sticking to a script. Also as a verb: to ad lib or ad libbing. "He prefers ad libbing to keeping to the text which makes life difficult for his fellow actors." Polite.

Light at the end of the tunnel
If there's light at the end of the tunnel it means that we can see the end of our present misery. "We've had a bad three years but now the economy is turning round there's light at the end of the tunnel." Polite.

Like a fish needs a bicycle
It is extremely difficult to imagine how a fish could ride a bicycle. So this is a concept of uselessness which is also a put-down. "Thank you for your advice. I need it like a fish needs a bicycle." Not really polite.

Living daylights
Living daylights are always knocked out of someone, never put in! It means that the person was knocked unconscious so he saw stars. "With a couple of blows to the jaw he knocked the living daylights out of him." Slang.

Long and short of it
This means taking everything into account. "He thinks he will be believed but when you look at the

evidence the long and the short of it is that he doesn't stand a chance." Polite.

Long chalk

To keep a running tally of winners and losers in a series of games or races the usual way is to mark four down-strokes and the fifth horizontal to make for easy counting. If one player is well ahead of his opponent his horizontal chalk line is longer. He is ahead by a long chalk. It is also used in the negative meaning that the game isn't over and the outcome is not yet clear. "Vettel is in the lead but he's not the winner yet – not by a long chalk." Polite.

Look-in

This has two meanings: 1) to visit within the building (office) or come round to a friend's house. "Next time you're in the village why not look in for a cup of tea!" and 2) an opportunity to participate (but usually in the negative). "They are a tight-knit group and when they are drinking together you don't get a look-in." Polite.

Look into

This doesn't involve the eyes but the brain. You look into something by giving it your attention and establishing the facts. "He came to me with a question about dog licences and I said I'd look into it for him." Polite.

Loose end

A knotted rope has a tied end and a loose end: the loose end is simply surplus rope. This translates metaphorically into having nothing of consequence on your agenda. "If you find you're at a loose end on Friday evening give me a ring and we'll go down to the pub together." Polite.

Lost his marbles
Small boys value playground marbles for their size and colour and to lose one is a tragedy. In later life the brain takes the place of the marbles so this is a metaphor for losing one's mental capacity. "Sad to say, I think Grandpa's losing his marbles. His speech is rambling and he finds it hard to stick to one subject for any length of time." Polite.

Lost his rag
This means lost his temper. Teething babies often have a piece of cloth as a comforter and if they lose it or throw it out of the pram they scream. Some grown men do the same - they lose their rag. "When he heard the bad news he lost his rag and blamed everyone but himself." Polite

Lost the plot
This is a phrase that relies on rhyme. If the teller of a story departs from the plot it may be because he's boring or because his brain isn't functioning - this implies the latter. "She's so unreliable these days that I think she's lost the plot." Polite.

M

Make a clean breast of
This means to confess to a mistake without offering any excuse. "If you've broken her favourite teapot the only thing you can do is make a clean breast of it. Putting it back in the cupboard is only storing up trouble for later." Polite.

Make a good fist
Fists are usually for fighting but here they are holding playing cards. To make a good fist is to plan and execute a series of moves that brings success at cards or simply to do something well. "She was given a hard task for which she had no experience but she made a good fist of it." Polite.

Make a killing/Make a fortune
To make a lot of money quickly from one or more transactions or investments. "He made a killing in

sugar that year. He bought at the bottom of the market and sold almost at the top". If he had taken a lifetime to do this it would be, "He made his fortune in sugar." Polite.

Make common cause
When a group joins another group with whom they are not usually associated solely to promote an idea or argument they make common cause. "Teachers and farm workers share few aspirations but they make common cause when seeking to raise the national minimum wage." Polite.

Make do and mend
This was a World War II slogan when clothes and household utensils were in very short supply and alliteration was not. Today it is more usual to hear only the first half of the saying. "We've run out of porridge oats. We'll just have to make do with cereal until I go to the shops on Thursday." Polite.

Make your number
To make your number with someone you have to be recognised by them for having done good work. "If you want to get on in this place you have to make your number with Fred. A bunch of flowers for his secretary is not enough! Fred needs results!" Polite.

Man of many parts
This is a person with a number of different talents or interests. It is often used in eulogies. "He was not just an engineer: he was a man of many parts - a mason, a sailor and a hill walker as well as pulling his weight on the Council." Polite.

Manner of speaking
This has nothing to do with accent or intonation but means that the description given is comparable to different but similar situation. "The Church wouldn't marry them because he's divorced even though he was the innocent party. It's like Peter Townsend and Princess Margaret, in a manner of speaking." Polite.

Mea culpa
This is a rather grand admission of blame: Latin = my fault. "Tom is very stubborn and can't see that he's done wrong. The last thing he's going to do is issue a mea culpa." Polite.

Met his Maker
We meet our Maker when we die and have to give an account of ourselves. The implication of this alliterative phrase is more on the former than the latter. "He met his Maker sooner than he expected – the consequence of driving too fast on a slippery road." Polite.

Mind your own business
This is an order not to interfere in another's life or interests. "He meant well but she misunderstood his good intentions and told him firmly to mind his own business." Not really polite.

Mind your Ps and Qs
Today publicans don't give credit but when they did the beer was chalked up on a board as Pints and Quarts. (English beer was not very strong). So mind your Ps and Qs means behaving yourself and, in particular, speaking carefully about a subject. "He was

rather flippant and this upset Aunt Agatha. She told him to mind his Ps and Qs." Polite.

Miss is as good as a mile
This originates in cricket but now is used more widely. The bowler's aim is to hit the wicket the batsman is protecting. The ball may whistle past the wicket but if it misses it doesn't matter to the batsman whether it is by a hair's breadth or half a metre – a miss is as good as a mile. The same applies when used in any circumstances where hitting the target is critical. "He promised to be early and was only two minutes late but in her eyes a miss is as good as a mile. He was late and that was that." Polite.

Money for jam/old rope
When there's easy profit to be made with minimal effort it is money for jam or money for old rope. Old rope is unreliable as a mooring or tether. It has to be carted away for sale but is probably free to the buer so any proceeds are pure profit. Money for jam means that there will be something sweet to put on the bread. "She has flair and the materials cost her pennies so making expensive hats for sale is money for jam for her." Polite.

Month of Sundays
Every month has 4 or 5 Sundays but none has 30 or 31. So this expression means extremely unlikely. "He's madly in love with her but she wouldn't marry him in a month of Sundays." Polite.

Moot point
This is a matter that can be argued in different ways

and therefore worthy of serious debate. "It is a moot point whether the world's rise in temperature is caused mainly by human activity or by long-term weather cycles." Polite.

Motherhood and apple pie
When a politician doesn't want to upset voters he speaks about things on which everyone agrees and no-one would vote against such as motherhood. "He had nothing new to announce and what he said was all motherhood and apple pie." Polite.

Murphy's Law
This "law" states that if something can go wrong it will go wrong. (Murphy is a common Irish name and the English joke about the Irish). "Despite all his hard work he was the victim of Murphy's Law and the computer system crashed on its first outing." Polite.

N

Near the bone/Near the knuckle
Of a joke or expression this means bordering on the indecent – definitely not drawing room or mixed company humour. It is possibly derived from the expression "the meat is sweetest near the bone." "He is always funny but you must be careful who you introduce him to, as his humour is often near the bone." Polite.

Neck of the woods
Woods are rarely narrow like a neck: this is possibly a corruption of the Dutch "hoek" meaning corner. In the neck of the woods means in the neighbourhood or locality whether in town or country. "If you happen to be in our neck of the woods give us a ring and come round for supper." Polite.

Needle in a haystack
It is difficult to understand why a needle should be in a haystack but one thing is sure – if you drop it you'll have great difficulty finding it. "We had to find that man before dawn but with nothing to go on and the whole of London as our territory it was like looking for a needle in a haystack." Polite.

Nimby
An acronym for "Not in my backyard" – a nimby is a person who supports proposals as long as they don't impinge on his own life or property e.g. a new road or housing estate is good as long as it is not near him. "We need this road desperately but it goes through suburbs that are full of nimbys and they all have votes." Polite.

Nineteen to the dozen
A dozen is 12 and 19 is a lot bigger than that. This usually refers to mechanical or operational speed. "They were going nineteen to the dozen to get the job done because they didn't want to have to work overtime on a Friday." Polite.

No rhyme or reason
Alliteration predominates here! What can rhyme and reason have in common? One is romantic and the other rational. Also this is always used negatively to mean that there is no justification for the action described. "There is no rhyme or reason why she can't be present at her aunt's wedding. She's just making excuses." Polite.

No uncertain terms
This means in words that cannot be ignored or forgotten. "I told him in no uncertain terms that he was not to phone my daughter again otherwise I'd call the police." Polite.

Nod and a wink
If you give someone a nod and a wink you are imparting secret information. It may between you and the auctioneer to raise your bid or with a friend about an opportunity. "Whenever he saw an opportunity he'd give me a nod and a wink." Polite.

Nose in the air
If you don't want to "see" someone you can walk past gazing into the sky as if looking for a rare bird or studying the cloud formation and your nose will be in the air. The unseen person will use your posture to describe you to his friends. "He looked right through me and walked past with his nose in the air". Not very polite.

Nose out of joint
To have one's nose put out of joint means to be discredited or humiliated. So it refers to other people not to oneself! Speaking about yourself you'd say "I was upset" but speaking of the other chap, "His nose was put out of joint when he heard that she had accepted my invitation and declined his." Polite.

Nose to the grindstone
This sounds more painful than it is which is to keep on working hard at a job or problem, either from self-motivation or because it is required. "He has a big

problem to solve and his boss is keeping his nose to the grindstone until he's solved it." Polite.

Not cricket
Most cricket takes place on village greens between club sides and there is a code of conduct that says if the batsman knows he is out he "walks" i.e. goes back to the pavilion. That is cricket. Not cricket is to disobey that code. In everyday life "not cricket" is not behaving with total integrity. "He knows very well he's in the wrong and not admitting it is just not cricket." Polite.

Not just a pretty face
Some ladies may improve their employment prospects if they are good looking e.g. receptionists. But they also need skills to do the job well so it is important that they are not just a pretty face. The wider expression indicates competence as well as presence and can be used of either sex. "He's a qualified plumber. He's not just a pretty face." Polite.

Now and again
This means occasionally or infrequently and is best explained by a limerick which tells the opposite. "There was a young lady called Jane, Who liked to kiss now and again. Not now and again, But now and again, And again and again and again." Polite.

Now and then
This also means occasionally, not often. "We come past your door now and then. Next time we'll let you know and perhaps we can do something together." Polite.

O

Odds-on

When bookmakers (bookies) at a racecourse shout the odds on horses they do so as "10 to 1" or "7 to 2". In other words you bet £1 and if you win you get back £10 plus your stake. But sometimes there is a clear favourite and because of the weight of money placed the odds can be reversed so they are, say, 2 to 7 which is referred to as "7 to 2 on" which means that you bet £7 to win £2 plus your stake. This is said to be "odds-on" and can be used whenever the result looks certain. "He's the odds-on favourite for the job. He is, after all, the boss's son-in-law." Polite.

Off with the old and on with the new

Originally relating to wearing new clothes, this is an expression critical of someone who discards an existing practice when a new one is offered, regardless of whether the old still has uses. "When the new computer arrived it was off with the old and on with the new but the new machine is programmed differently and we've lost a lot of data." Polite.

Old bean

This is a dated jocular greeting (man to man) between friends of a certain age. It also describes a pompous person who would use the expression. "Good to see you, old bean, how are you?" or "He's a bit of an old bean." Polite.

Old habits die hard

When habits are ingrained and of long standing it is difficult to change them - old habits die hard. "Even though we have portable phones older people still go to the sideboard where the phone lives. Often, because the phone is portable nowadays, it isn't there and they can't find it." Polite.

Old hat

There is no logic in this expression. It simply means out of date thinking that has been superseded. "He suggested the Nazi movement was stimulated by Wagner's operas but the critic said that was old hat and the truth was that it was only Hitler's personal love of the music that made Wagner fashionable." Polite.

On the game

Ladies who sell their favours are said to be "on the game." Today we call them "sex workers" which is much less glamorous. "She's a single girl with many men friends who she often entertains overnight. I have to assume she's on the game." Polite.

On the hook
This means committed to a course of action. "If you can persuade them to buy this computer they'll be on the hook for all the upgrades and maintenance charges." Polite.

On the off chance
This means taking a gamble on the outcome of an action. There is no "on chance". "I came round on the off chance that you might be free this evening and we could go out for a drink." Polite.

On the ropes
If a boxer holds on to the ropes it is an admission that he cannot stand and has therefore lost the fight. By analogy if a person or institution is on the ropes he or it has come to the end of its time. "His company folded and because he had given the bank personal guarantees that put him on the ropes as well." Polite.

On the side of the angels
In favour of all things good and kind, virtuous and long-suffering. "In public he's on the side of the angels but in committee he can be very narrow-minded and extremely stubborn." Polite.

On the tiles
This means a heavy night's drinking or partying. "I was out on the tiles last night and this morning I've a dreadful hangover." Polite.

On the wagon
In the nineteenth century the Temperance Movement would parade through a city with a horse-drawn

wagon carrying those who had signed the pledge to stop drinking. So to be on the wagon is to abstain from alcohol. "He used to be a heavy drinker but he's on the wagon for Lent. Whether he'll keep it up after Lent remains to be seen." Polite.

On the wing
While birds are always on the wing, this refers more to doing repairs (on airplanes) while in flight and so, by inference, coping with the unexpected while proceeding with normal work. "We have to start now so if you haven't finished checking everything we'll just have to do it on the wing." Polite.

On top of the world
Full of happiness and joy. "I'm on top of the world looking down on creation And the only explanation I can find Is the love that I've found ever since you've been around Your love's put me at the top of the world" The Carpenters or "When he got his exam results he was on top of the world." Polite.

One for the road
Before cars and drink/drive when the horse knew its way home, it was customary to offer your guest a last drink to keep him warm on his journey and this would be the expression to use. "In an effort to keep him longer because he talks so cogently I offered him one for the road but he declined graciously and slipped into the back of his chauffeur-driven car." Polite.

One hand tied behind your back
If restrictions are placed on your actions making it

difficult to achieve your objective you have one hand tied behind your back. "He was happy to take on the investigation but he was not allowed to interview any of the parties involved under oath so from the start he was working with one hand tied behind his back". Polite.

Or so
This is a useful approximation of quantity or time and avoids having to be precise. "There were a hundred or so people present at the meeting." Polite.

Out for the count
A boxing term for when a fighter is on the floor for more than the count of 10. Also applied to a heavy sleeper. "He was out for the count after his business lunch so I crept out and did my shopping." Polite.

Out of his depth
If a person is intellectually unable to understand an argument he is out of his depth in that subject. "He may be a brilliant physicist but when it comes to economics he's soon out of his depth." Polite.

Out of order
A formal meeting has an agenda and it is usual to take its items in order. Being out of order means breaching this or other conventions and breaking the rules. "In my view he's out of order raising that private topic when non-members are present." Polite.

Out of sorts
Bad news, bad health or bad weather can all put any of us out of sorts – we become negative and

pessimistic, uncertain about life in general. "He sometimes suffers from acute indigestion and it really puts him out of sorts." Polite.

Out of the blue

If the sky is blue and the sun shining it is difficult to see falling objects or enemy aircraft coming from behind. Something that comes out of the blue is unexpected and mostly not pleasant. "She was all set for a romantic long weekend when out of the blue he announced he was going skiing with an old school friend over Easter." Polite.

Over-egg the pudding

Making the subject look much better than it really is: the glaze on top is better than the pudding underneath. By inference giving only the good points of a proposal and being too enthusiastic. "The idea is sound and it will save money but we must be careful not to over-egg the pudding." Polite.

P

Pain in the neck
No-one likes a pain in the neck whether it's physical or metaphorical. "He's a bore, he only talks about himself and he goes on and on about the same old thing. In short he's a pain in the neck!" Polite.

Part and parcel
Another alliteration that the English love. The parcel here is not a box you send through the post but a piece of land attached to a larger piece. By inference it means of the same type. "The demonstrators may be a different crowd but they are part and parcel of the same movement." Polite.

Past master
Formally a past master is someone who has previously held the rank of Master in a college or masonic lodge. Informally it is anyone who is an

expert in his field which may be technical or social. "From the age of two he was a past master at getting his own way with his mother: he just bawled his head off until she gave in." Polite.

Pay through the nose

Pay more for goods or services than expected or justified. "If he doesn't settle his account soon I'll make him pay through the nose the next time he wants to use our service." Polite.

PDQ

PDQ is short for "Pretty damn quick" – slightly imitating the subjected races (especially the Chinese). It is a bit peremptory but between friends or family it is a way of saying "Get on with it. Do it now." "I'm in a hurry to get on the road so please load up the car PDQ." Polite between friends but can be aggressive.

Pear-shaped

When something goes pear-shaped it goes badly wrong. Presumably (in the mind of the speaker) the original pear was supposed to be shaped like an orange but became elongated. "When the dam was sanctioned it was assumed that construction costs would remain low but they have risen with inflation and the economics of the project have gone pear-shaped." Polite.

Penny dropped

Public toilets in Britain used to be opened by putting a penny in a slot to release the lock. The mechanisms were often slow so you had to wait for the penny to drop before the door would unlock. The meaning of the phrase has developed to mean taking a long time to realise what the speaker is talking about. "I tried to explain the offside rule but he just couldn't get the hang of it until suddenly the penny dropped." Polite.

Perish the thought!
This is a conventional way of correcting a misunderstanding by the hearer who queries the meaning of a remark. "I asked her whether her grandmother was still with them. She said, 'Do you mean has she died?' 'Perish the thought,' I said. 'What I meant was has she gone back to her own home or is she still staying with you since her illness'." Polite.

Peter out
To come (slowly) to an end. Used about a seam of coal or mineral but also about human activities. "There was a lot of support initially but it petered out when the polls showed the majority of the public were against it." Polite.

Philistine
To the ancient Jews their neighbours the Philistines were uncultivated. This epithet has been extended to mean anyone who doesn't care for civilised things especially art or classical music. "He loves traditional jazz but when it comes to classical music he's a complete philistine." Polite.

Piece of cake
A task that is difficult for an unskilled person may be easy for a properly trained one. Why piece of cake? Presumably because it's easy to eat. "Once you've got the hang of it, milking a cow is a piece of cake but it's

tough on the forearms." Slang.

Pig's ear
Derives from the expression, "You can't make a silk purse out of a sow's ear". It means making a mess of doing something. "I asked him to count the cash but he made a pig's ear of it and I had to do it myself". Not really polite.

Pipe down
This is what you say to young people who are making too much noise. The origin is the call in the navy to go to your bunk beds for the night. The sound of the bosun's whistle is high like that of a young person. "It's gone 10 o'clock. It's time to pipe down and go to sleep." Quite polite.

Pipped at the post
When a runner leads throughout a race but is beaten in the closing stage he is pipped at the post. Metaphorically the same applies when a presumed certain outcome proves at the last minute not to happen. "Hillary Clinton looked like a certain winner but she was pipped at the post by Donald Trump." Polite.

Plain sailing
Sailing among rocks and shoals requires skill but in open water it is easier. Plain sailing means the latter and can be used in any context. "Once he's got the foundation laid putting up the shed will be plain sailing." Polite. ✓

Play box and cox
Box and Cox were two characters in Victorian music hall who used the same lodging room, one working on night shift and the other during the day. Today it can apply to job-sharing or any situation where two people fulfil one task. "Arranging the flowers in church I play box and cox with Mary – we do alternate Sundays." Polite.

Play second fiddle
The first violin is the leader of the orchestra and the first violins play the tune. The second violins play the harmony so do not attract the same attention. Playing second fiddle is a supporting role with little recognition. "Throughout their married lives he played second fiddle to his wife." Polite.

Play to the gallery
The gallery is the topmost tier of the audience with the cheapest seats and, by inference, the least sophistication. So to play to the gallery means to get cheap laughs at the expense of quality acting. "He speaks well but his failing is that he enjoys playing to the gallery more than giving a serious talk." Polite.

Plays with a straight bat
The wicket in cricket consists of three vertical stumps with bails on top and this has to be defended. As it is a vertical target a good batsman keeps his bat vertical and doesn't hit across the line of the ball. He plays with a straight bat. By inference he is a good guy, stylish, honest, reliable and trustworthy. "Throughout his working life he always played with a straight bat." Polite.

Pleased as Punch

Punch is a character in a Punch and Judy show and has a large and permanent smile even when he's hitting Judy over the head with his truncheon. Alliteration helps this simple phrase. "He came into the room with a large grin on his face looking pleased as Punch." Polite.

Poppycock

This is a not very polite way of saying that someone is talking rubbish. "He believes in what he's saying but it's all poppycock to me." Not really polite.

Pot boiler

Not all a novelist's output is uniform: sometimes a book has to be written to meet a publisher's schedule or other deadline. If this shows in the writing critics will say that the book is a pot boiler. It is written to earn royalties rather than from inspiration. "I enjoyed his first three books but in my view this one is a pot boiler." Polite.

Pot calling the kettle black

On a coal-fired cooking range all the cooking vessels get soot on their under sides and no one more than the other. So for the pot to call the kettle black is to see fault in others that you cannot see in yourself. "For her to say her neighbour gossips is just the pot calling the kettle black – as evidenced by her own remark." Polite.

Potty

This is a slightly old-fashioned expression meaning mildly eccentric (as in elderly maiden aunts) or overly enthusiastic (as in young lovers). "My aunt is potty about aspidistras and has at least a dozen in her house." Or "He's potty about her but she has other boyfriends and is just happy to receive his attentions." Polite.

Pound to a pinch of salt
Dressed up as a bet, this says that you are certain of what you say and are prepared to stake long odds that you are right. "A pound to a pinch of salt Henry will propose to Sheila while they're on their skiing holiday." Polite.

Prick up his ears
Attract the attention of the hearer. "He was not interested in what I had to say until I mentioned the plan to develop the land opposite his house. That made him prick up his ears." Polite.

Pull the other one
To pull someone's leg is to tease them or persuade them of something that is unlikely. This reply shows that you are aware of that fact. "He said that Navratilova would easily beat Bartol but she said 'Pull the other one!'" Not quite polite.

Push comes to shove
If the car goes into the ditch it may be possible to push it out but if not you may have to shove by putting your shoulder to it. Metaphorically it means when circumstances are extreme. "If push comes to shove we'll just have to cut the workforce." Polite.

Push off
A peremptory and rude exhortation to go away. "The salesman kept coming back hoping to get an order but I told him to push off." Impolite.

Push the boat out
To make a proposal, initiate cooperation or show hospitality especially when it's unexpected. "He wanted to get to know the new neighbours so he pushed the boat out and invited them round for drinks on Sunday morning." Polite.

Put all your eggs in one basket
Bad idea if you drop the basket! Similarly with investments, for example, it's not a good idea to have all your eggs in one basket – one industry, one product or one geographical area. "If you put all your eggs in one basket you risk losing everything if things goes wrong." Polite.

Put on the spot
Called to account or challenged – think football when the referee picks up the ball and puts it on the penalty spot. "I had decided to vote against his plan but he put me on the spot by asking where I'd got the information that made me change my mind." Polite.

Put paid to
To put paid to something is to bring it to a conclusion. The origin is settling a bill and stamping it 'Paid' before filing it. "Her strong personality and charisma put paid to any plan I had to stand against her in the forthcoming election." Polite.

Put two and two together
Alliteration helps to emphasise that this is a logical deduction from the facts presented. "He arrives late, is out of breath and looks untidy. Putting two and two together I'd say his car has broken down again." Polite.

Put up with
This means to tolerate a person or situation. "He may not like his manager but he has either to put up with him or find another job." Polite.

Put upon
To be subjected to unwelcome pressure. "He didn't really want to go skiing but his brother insisted he did as the bookings had been made. He felt put upon as this had been done without consulting him." Polite.

Put your money where your mouth is
If you really believe in something you don't just talk about it you commit yourself to it. It doesn't have to be a money investment: it could be to give it your time and effort. "He's always talking about that charity but he does nothing to help them. He should put his money where his mouth is." Polite.

Q

Queer as a coot

"Queer" is a tricky word: it can be either quite acceptable or highly pejorative. "I'm feeling a bit queer" might mean dizzy, faint or with an upset tummy but "queer" also means homosexual. So to say of a man that he is queer as a coot labels him either as a homosexual or because of his manner. It is easily mistaken and can cause offence. A coot is a small water bird so this is simply alliteration. Impolite.

Quid

A quid is slang for one pound Sterling. "I'll bet you five quid he wins the next race." Note that it is never plural. Also do not confuse this with "quid pro quo" which is Latin for "This thing for that thing" and is often used in the expression "All quid and no quo" meaning that the terms offered favour the proposer and offer too little to the other party. Polite.

R

Racing certainty
In horse-racing nothing is certain but in some races there is one outstanding horse that will almost certainly win. That is a racing certainty. "It's a racing certainty he'll be appointed. He didn't marry the boss' daughter for nothing." Polite.

Rag tag and bobtail
What's left when the good bits have been taken away. Generally used about people rather than things. "The procession was orderly at the beginning but descended into chaos as the rag, tag and bobtail came along." Polite.

Raining stair-rods
Stair rods are the straight rods used to hold the stair carpet in place. So rain that falls in stair rods is hard and not blown sideways by the wind. "We had

umbrellas but it was raining stair rods so we stayed inside until it eased off." Polite.

Rainy day

Savings are put aside for a rainy day i.e. if there should be a misfortune. "It's good to have a pension to look forward to but it's also good to have something put aside for a rainy day." Polite.

Read between the lines

The English are good at saying one thing and meaning another. So it's important to establish the real meaning and this may require reading between the lines to discover the truth. "Mother said that Aunt Jane wasn't angry with me for not writing to thank her for my present but reading between the lines I think she was upset and so was Aunt Jane." Polite.

Recruiting sergeant

The recruiting sergeant was the man who persuaded poor men of the advantages of joining the army. Politically the meaning has moved on to suggesting policies that will encourage voters to back the other side. "Raising taxes simply to pay off the national debt will be a recruiting sergeant for the opposition." Polite.

Red herring

This is a false clue or diversionary argument designed to confuse. "He suggested we start by looking in the house but this proved to be a red herring and we found the evidence we needed in the garden." Polite.

Right as rain
This is simply alliteration and has nothing to do with the weather. It refers to a person surviving an incident or to an ailment that has been cured. If a man falls off his bicycle, gets up and shakes himself down, a bystander might say "Give him a few minutes and he'll be right as rain." Polite.

Ring the changes
This refers originally to church bell ringing for which there are still competitions in rural England. There may be 8 or more bells that are rung in logical and changing sequences. In common speech it means doing a routine thing differently. If you're planning the annual garden party you might ask, "What can we do to ring the changes on last year?" Polite.

Rob Peter to pay Paul
This is a phrase of great antiquity that pre-dates the traditional explanation of selling the investments of Westminster Abbey (St Peter's) to pay for the rebuilding of St Paul's Cathedral after the Fire of London in 1666. Thus it means that if a group or organisation needs money it does not solve its problem by taking from one part and giving to another. Polite.

Root and branch (reform)
If you prune the branches of a shrub or tree and at the same time prune the roots you reduce the future growth of the plant substantially. So root and branch reform is radical reorganization. "The new chairman promised shareholders that there would be a root and branch reorganisation of the company as soon as he

had established his authority." Polite.

Rough diamond
Before a diamond is cut and polished it looks nothing but still has value. The same applies to a person who has practical skills and abilities but lacks social skills. "Our builder is a bit of a rough diamond but he did an excellent job on our roof." Polite.

Round the bend
You cannot see what is happening round the bend in the road so you should drive accordingly. Similarly with a person whose ideas are unusual or illogical – you treat his opinions with care. "You mustn't take him too seriously: he's completely round the bend on the subject of Europe." Polite.

Row of beans
A row of beans (not the plants) has no value as far as this expression is concerned. "Let's not argue about it. It's not worth a row of beans who is right and I'm not going to fall out with you over it." Polite.

Rub their nose in it
It used to be thought that you could train a puppy not to relieve himself in the house by rubbing his nose in the result. This has been transported to cover anyone who acts so unkindly on another's misfortune or incompetence. "The outing was not a success but she didn't have to rub the organiser's nose in it." Polite.

Ruffled feathers
Birds spend a lot of time preening and do not like having their feathers ruffled. So do pompous people.

"I thought I was being tactful but it seems I ruffled his feathers with my views on corporal punishment!"
Polite.

S

Savvy
Knowledgeable or street-wise. It is a corruption of the French "savoir" – to know, and arose from our troops' exposure in WW1. "He may look slow but when it comes to car engines he's pretty savvy." Polite.

Scalded cat
If a cat is scalded with hot water it rushes away and hides. So "He shot out of the room like a scalded cat" means he had embarrassed himself and couldn't wait to excuse himself or find a proper pretext to leave. Polite.

Scraping the barrel
This refers to the contents not the barrel – making sure that you have every last bit of it including any sediment that hasn't run out. By extension it means

bringing forward the weakest of arguments in support of a proposition. "He made some good points in favour of the proposal but towards the end I thought he was scraping the barrel." Polite.

Scruff of the neck
The scruff is the back of the neck of a small animal which is used to lift or drag it. Traditionally policemen or teachers took hold of small boys by the scruff of the neck (but no longer, of course). It is applied metaphorically to problems that require a vigorous solution. "Colleagues had shied away from dealing with the question of timetabling. What it needed was for someone to get hold of it by the scruff of the neck and thrash out a solution with the whole staff. He did and it worked." Polite.

Scuppered
A scupper is a hole in the side of a ship designed to release shipped water. When a vessel is sunk deliberately it is scuppered by opening these vents. By analogy this applies to any plan that fails because a part doesn't work. "If the engineering is faulty the whole project will be scuppered." Polite.

Seen and not heard
Children in Victorian times were expected to be seen and not heard. Happily we live in more enlightened times but the expression endures when the noise gets too much. "When I was a child," said her frustrated father, "children were seen and hot heard. So please turn the TV down so I can read my book in peace." Polite.

Send to Coventry
Why Coventry? It originated in the story of Lady Godiva who rode naked through the town to persuade her husband to reduce taxes on the townsfolk, all of whom looked the other way out of respect except for one Peeping Tom. No-one ever spoke to him afterwards. "They all agreed to keep it secret but she told the authorities so they sent her to Coventry." Polite.

Shaggy dog story
A long and repetitive story with a lot of irrelevant detail that ends in an anti-climax. "We heard a lot from him but it sounds more like a shaggy dog story than a coherent explanation." Polite.

Shake a stick at
This expression has no meaning other than to convey the idea of a number larger than the hearer may expect. "There are more potholes in that road than you can shake a stick at." Polite

Shank's pony
Shank's pony doesn't exist! It's your own two legs. "Going by shank's pony" simply means walking. The origin is that the shank is the shin bone between the knee and the ankle – hence you have to use your own legs. "I haven't got the bus fare so if I can't hitch a lift I'll just have to go by shank's pony." Polite.

Shedloads
A popular expression for a large amount – it could be of data but more usually money. The origin is unknown but it might be a throwback to the

comedian Tony Hancock who, in one sketch, takes a job as a builder's mate because the pay is very generous. When he asks what that shed in the corner is, the foreman replies, "That's not a shed, mate, it's your hod." Polite. (*Hod – a box on a short pole used for carrying bricks or tiles up a ladder to the builder or roofer.*)

Ship-shape
The full expression is "ship-shape and Bristol fashion" – Bristol being an important port in the West of England and closest to the Americas. It was renowned for its smartness so if everything, whether nautical or not, is ship-shape it is all orderly and in place. "It took me the whole morning to get the garage ship-shape again." Polite

Shit hit the fan
"Shit" is a coarse Anglo-Saxon word for what goes in the toilet pan. We all do it but we don't talk about it. It's also smelly. So, figuratively, when the shit hits the (electric) fan it spreads fast and everyone is tainted. This is a jocular expression for when the person on high wants to blame everyone for a calamity and vent his fury on all present. "When the Prime Minister heard the by-election results the shit hit the fan and the next Cabinet meeting was difficult." Impolite.

Shoot in the foot
This expression arose in World War 1 when a soldier could escape from the trenches by shooting himself in the foot. That was a deliberate act and it is still the correct meaning although today it is more often misused. Now it means to do damage to your case inadvertently. "He shot himself in the foot when it

slipped out that he hadn't worked late but had been in the pub He'd promised to come straight home from work so that they could go to the cinema." Polite.

Short commons
Short commons are scanty rations – insufficient food to maintain a healthy diet. "After he lost his job the family were on short commons until he found work again." Polite.

Shot my bolt
The crossbow fires a sharp and deadly bolt or arrow but it takes a long time to rewind to fire a second bolt. So with a crossbow you probably have only one shot and when you've shot your bolt you're vulnerable. Today it means that he's done all he can and has nothing more to offer. "He played like a demon for the first 30 minutes but by half-time he'd shot his bolt and had to be replaced." Polite.

Silly Billy
A gentle admonishment e.g. from mother to child when he's had an accident. It is not serious but very patronising between adults unless they are good friends. "He was adamant that he was right but his wife told him not to be a silly billy." Polite.

Sine qua non
Latin meaning "without which not" – in other words an essential ingredient for success. Pronounced "sinee quway none", it is slightly pompous in the wrong company. "He said it was a sine qua non that there would be formal speeches and vote of thanks after the dinner. Otherwise the meal had no purpose."

Polite.

Sing for your supper
If a person is invited to an event and asked to make a speech or propose a toast he sings for his supper – not literally but figuratively. "I was surprised to receive an invitation until I realised I would be asked to speak. They wanted me to sing for my supper." Polite.

Six of one and half-a-dozen of the other
Half-a-dozen is 6 so they are the same thing. "If you go by train it takes 40 minutes. You can drive it in 30 but then you have to find parking which will take at least 10 minutes. It's six of one and half-a-dozen of the other." Polite.

Sixes and sevens
This means to be in a muddle or in dispute. The origin lies in the London livery companies (the craft guilds that governed trading and manufacture of goods in cities in the Middle Ages) who had an order of precedence. This was disputed and in 1515 the Court of Aldermen in London decided as follows 1) Mercers, 2) Grocers, 3) Drapers, 4) Fishmongers, 5) Goldsmiths, but here they had a problem as 6) and 7) were disputed between the Merchant Taylors and the Skinners. The aldermen solved it by alternating the order each year! "He's at sixes and sevens about whether he's expected to attend the meeting." It is also a polite way of saying two people are in a mild dispute. "They're at sixes and sevens with each other." Polite.

Skin of the teeth
Teeth don't have any skin so to do something by the skin of your teeth is to just achieve your objective by the narrowest of margins. "It was an ambitious project but he achieved it by the skin of his teeth." Polite.

Slope off
This is a softer variant of "slink off" which has furtive connotations. "If the replay is on Wednesday afternoon we could slope off together to watch the match. No-one would notice our absence." Polite.

Slowly but surely
This alliteration means a step-by-step progress towards a desired end. "He was uncertain of any woman's ability to do the job but she is very efficient and slowly but surely she gained his confidence." Polite.

Smell a rat
Rats nesting under the floorboards smell: they are unhygienic and spread disease. So to smell a rat is to discover something nasty. "She listened carefully to the salesman's patter but she could smell a rat and asked a lot of awkward questions before deciding not to buy." Polite.

Snail's pace
Going very slowly as snails do. This relies on rhyme for its effect. "The traffic was solid and for more than an hour we were moving at a snail's pace." Polite.

Sold a pup
When puppies are small they are cute and it's not easy to see how big and ugly they may grow. This expression implies that it is an ugly mongrel not a pedigree dog. It means I am disappointed with my purchase. (Note that you never buy a pup – you are always sold one!). "They all praised the Toyota but I bought one secondhand and, frankly, I was sold a pup. It had obviously been abused by previous owners and was leaky and starting was unreliable." Polite.

Song and dance
To disagree or get upset about something the speaker thinks is trivial. "It's nothing special so why are you making a song and dance about it?" Polite. √

Spanner in the works
If a spanner drops between two moving cogs it can cause a lot of damage and even bring the machine to a halt. Metaphorically the spanner is anything that ruins a plan. "His insistence on demanding a vote threw a spanner in the works for the Prime Minister, who was expecting to go ahead without seeking the consent of Parliament." Polite.

Spend a penny
A term ladies use for going to the toilet. It originates from the days when you had to put a penny in the slot to release the door lock on a public toilet. "Excuse me for a moment while I spend a penny." Polite.

Spike their guns
One of the light cavalry's tasks in a battle was to ride

down fast to the enemy's cannon, overpower the gun crew and hammer a spike into the firing hole to disable the gun. So spiking his guns is disabling a competitor's advantages. "If we lower our prices that will spike his guns because his overheads are higher than ours and he can't afford to match us." Polite.

Spill the beans

This means to tell the story. "Come on, spill the beans" means "Tell me the facts", especially when something has gone wrong and the speaker wants to find out why. "To save his own skin he spilt the beans about our plot to bomb the warehouse." Polite.

Spin a yarn

Before the invention of the spinning jenny women spun fibres by hand into thread (or yarn) usually in the company of other women. Naturally they told stories among themselves (which became yarns) but if they were far-fetched they might be accused of spinning a yarn. "I should take what he says with a pinch of salt. He's good at spinning a yarn." Polite.

Sprat to catch a mackerel

This is a small concession granted by one side to gain a larger one in return. "We are conceding the permission to build in the side street provided they grant us the right to build on the main square. It's a sprat to catch a mackerel." Polite.

Stands out like a sore thumb

A wounded thumb hurts and limits one's grip: it is an obvious nuisance. Similarly, an obstacle that patently threatens the success of a proposal is a nuisance. "It stands out like a sore thumb that if her father is opposed to any marriage at all and she is intent on obeying him then she's going to remain a spinster." Polite.

Step on the gas
Gas is short for gasoline in America (petrol in England). So to step on the gas is to put your foot down on the accelerator and drive fast. "We were late so there was nothing for it but to step on the gas. We got there but it wasn't fun." Polite.

Step up to the plate
An American expression from baseball meaning to become the next batsman/runner. By implication it means to shoulder responsibility. "In my view it's time he stepped up to the plate and took on this responsibility." Polite.

Sticky wicket
Strictly "He's batting on a sticky wicket" which comes from cricket. When it rains and then turns sunny and hot the grass wicket dries out quickly and a spin bowler can turn the ball dramatically on the bounce. This makes it massively difficult for the batsman to play – he's on a sticky wicket. By inference, it relates to situations where success is required from an almost impossible task. "He's promised he'll succeed but the task keeps on getting bigger. He's on a very sticky wicket." Polite.

Straight from the shoulder
This means to tell bad news without softening the blow or making excuses. "I knew how the losses

arose in his business and I gave it to him straight from the shoulder which of his employees were dishonest and how they were defrauding him." Polite

Streets ahead

This means much better or more competent than another person or group. "He's streets ahead of me in maths though I'm better than he is at languages." Polite.

Stretch a point

To stretch a point is to apply an argument beyond its proper application. "We agree that cars pollute the air and are a danger to pedestrians but it is stretching a point to say that they should therefore be banned from all high streets." Polite.

Stuck up

A person who is stuck up fancies himself and consequently may be rude to those he considers his inferiors. "He has no breeding or manners at all! He's so stuck up he'll only speak to you if he wants something from you." Polite.

Sub judice

As a legal term it means that the matter is within the jurisdiction of the court and therefore cannot be commented on without risking being in contempt of court. It has a less exalted meaning when applied to circumstances other than court hearings meaning that a decision on how to proceed is still under consideration. "We all know he has defrauded the company but what action the board will take is still sub judice." Polite.

Sunk without trace

While this derives from unfortunate circumstances – the sinking of a vessel – it has acquired a more general sense that a person (or subject) who was previously prominent has disappeared from view leaving no evidence of their previous presence. "For months after the Profumo affair Christine Keeler was never out of the papers. Then she sank without trace when the public lost interest." Polite.

Sure as hell

Hell is a certainty for sinners so something that is as sure as hell is definitely going to happen. "He's very determined to succeed and sure as hell he will in the end." Barely polite.

Sure-fire

A sure-fire thing is a certainty – a course of action that is guaranteed success. "One sure-fire way to get a date with her is to send her a bunch of flowers with an invitation to the theatre." Polite.

Sweep under the carpet

Before the days of fitted carpets dust from the borders could be disposed of (temporarily) by sweeping it under the carpet. This now applies to an embarrassment one wants to hide. "The Tories are better at sweeping their mistakes under the carpet than the Labour Party who tend to go on arguing about them." Polite.

Swing the lead

To measure the depth of the water a sailor would be posted at the bow of a sailing ship to swing a lead-weighted rope into the sea every few hundred yards. Hauling it in was hard work and if he could pretend to swing the lead without releasing it a lazy sailor could avoid the heavy work. So this means avoiding responsibility by pretending sickness or another excuse not to participate. "If he fancies a day off he's not above swinging the lead and putting in a sick note." Polite.

T

Tail wags the dog
Dogs wag their tails when they are happy but the tail is smaller than the dog. If the tail wags the dog it means that a dominant minority rules the subservient majority. "The French may own only 30% of the company but try implementing anything new without their support and you'll find the tail wags the dog." Polite

Take for granted
This has two meanings that are slightly different 1) it is a given or an immutable assumption or 2) he is unacknowledged or not thanked. "He took it for granted that I would go to the cinema with him." or "No-one likes to be taken for granted and she would appreciate a small gesture of thanks." Polite.

Take hostages
Note that this is always plural and it is metaphorical not actual. It means that an argument is put forward crushingly and allowing no room for compromise or discussion. "He's very sure of himself and when he argues his case he doesn't take hostages." Polite.

Take up the cudgels
To support someone in a disagreement. Obviously originally a physical fight (cudgels = clubs) but nowadays it is more likely to be in a social, intellectual or business disagreement. "He took up the cudgels on her behalf when she was being bullied by her neighbour." Polite.

Taken for a ride
This means to be misled or cheated. "I don't trust that greengrocer. I've been taken for a ride more than once and sold poor vegetables from the back of the stand." Polite.

Taking the mickey
The expression "taking the piss" is not polite but this Cockney rhyming slang version (based on a mythical character Mickey Bliss) is acceptable. It means teasing or exaggerating a person's characteristics or opinions to make fun of him. "He has such extreme views in favour of capital punishment that I suggested he should try it out on himself but he realised I was taking the mickey and retorted "Perhaps I should murder you!" Polite.

Talk the hind leg off a donkey
Describes someone who is boring and monopolises

the conversation or never stops talking. "He may be shy but get him going on his wartime experiences flying in Bomber Command and he'll talk the hind leg off a donkey." Polite.

Tea in China
There is a lot of tea in China so used as a measure of dislike it stands high. "She had told her friends she wouldn't go out with him for all the tea in China. So it was a surprise to see them dancing together." Polite.

Teach your grandmother to suck eggs
To explain something that is obvious or to go to lengths to elaborate on something that the hearer knows already. "I'm not trying to teach my grandmother to suck eggs but the Charge of the Light Brigade happened because a junior officer misinterpreted his general's command." Polite.

Tell porkies
This means to tell lies (Cockney rhyming slang – pork pies = lies). It is a slightly disparaging way of saying that someone is not telling the whole truth. It can be jocular but can also be serious depending on the tone of voice. "I suggested that one or two of his statements were really porkies." Quite polite.

Thanks a bunch
No one knows what's in the bunch but whatever it is, it's unwelcome. This is a none-too-polite way of saying you've done me a disservice. "He bid the hand up to game and when he laid down his cards I had to say "Thank you partner" but what I really meant was "Thanks a bunch – you've given me a problem by

your over-bidding." Ironic and not really polite.

Thick and fast
This means with speed and in great numbers. "At Isandlwana the Zulus came over the hill thick and fast and fell on the British soldiers' camp. In two hours they killed more than 1400 men. It was a massacre." Polite.

Thick and thin
This means in good times and bad and refers especially to loyalty. "He stuck by his leader in opposition through thick and thin and was disappointed that his reward was no more than a minor post in government." Polite.

Thick as thieves
When friends bond closely they become thick as thieves. Thieves don't necessarily bond more than other men even if they steal together but the English love the alliteration. "The boys only met at the beginning of the school holidays but by the end of the summer they'd become thick as thieves." Polite.

Thick as two short planks
A short plank is as thick as a long plank and two are no thicker than one unless one lies on top of the other! Conventionally, "thick" means dim-witted so the expression means not just dim but very dim. "His poor performance is because he's as thick as two short planks." Rude.

Thick end
The larger part, especially of a sum of money. "I just

went out for a beer with him but by the end of the evening I'd spent the thick end of £30 because we went on to have supper together." Polite.

Think outside the box
To be creative and work from first principles rather than following existing practice. This is current and hackneyed management-speak and so best avoided! "He exhorted them to think outside the box but without giving them any leads or ideas of his own." Polite.

Thorn in the side
A thorn in the finger is inconvenient but a thorn in the side is a positive nuisance and much more painful. It has the semblance of a dagger or the spear that the Roman thrust into Christ's side. "Heseltine had always planned to be Prime Minister and throughout his time in Cabinet he was a thorn in Margaret Thatcher's side." Polite.

Throw the baby out with the bath water
Lose sight of the objective of a procedure in an effort to cover every eventuality. "By immunising every patient who arrived at the hospital the doctors threw the baby out with the bathwater by creating a backlog which delayed other treatments and resulted in longer hospitalisation." Polite.

Thumbnail sketch
You can't paint a detailed picture on a thumbnail but you can give an impression. So a thumbnail sketch concentrates on the highlights and ignores the detail. "We haven't a lot of time so just give us a thumbnail

sketch of what you're proposing." Polite.

Tickety-boo
This means all is well – a light-hearted expression. "We've had some problems with the central heating in the house but now everything's tickety-boo." Polite.

Tickle the fancy
Create enthusiasm or mild excitement (possibly, but not necessarily, with romantic overtones). "The idea of them going away to a hotel for the weekend tickled her fancy." Polite.

Tighten the belt
If times are hard and food is short we lose weight and our waists shrink. We have to tighten our belts to keep our trousers up. Metaphorically it means having to be more economical and live within our means. "There are fewer jobs and pay rates have gone down. People have to tighten their belts until the good times return." Polite.

Till kingdom come
This refers to the Christian belief that Jesus will return to earth to establish his kingdom. But that appears to be a long way into the future so the expression means for a very long time or forever. "Once he got started there was no stopping him and we thought he'd go on ranting till kingdom come." Polite.

Till the cows come home
The cows are in the field during the day but come in

for evening milking. But that's well in the future and if someone won't stop talking we say he'll go on till the cows come home. "If you start him off on the EU he'll go on till the cows come home." Polite.

Time is running out
When a deadline has to be met there is a limit to the time available to effect change: time is running out. "The Parliamentary session ends in two weeks' time so time is running out to make changes to the bill." Polite.

Tip off
A tip in this context is a nod in a particular direction – a favoured horse in a race or an investment on the Stock Exchange. "I was thinking of buying this share but he tipped me off to wait until after the next dividend payment when the share price might go down for a time." Polite.

To a T
Something that fits to a T, fits perfectly – it can be a garment or a description of an event or a person. "She took the little dress into the changing room and when she came out there was no doubt it fitted her to a T." Polite.

To no avail
Without success. "I spent half my life trying to persuade the children that it is better to be 10 minutes early than 5 minutes late but to no avail. They simply cannot keep time." Polite.

To your heart's content
This means repeating something until you have total satisfaction (or get bored). "The boy was enraptured by his present and played with it to his heart's content all afternoon." Polite.

Ton of bricks
A ton of stone weighs the same as a ton of bricks but the latter have a regularity that implies authority. They also have sharp edges. "Desmond started to argue but the chairman came down on him like a ton of bricks and shut him up." Polite.

Touch and go
The fuse on an explosive or firework is called the touch-paper. You light it and have a short time to get away. "If you don't come soon it will be touch and go whether we make the train." Polite.

Trial and error
When there is no logical process one can only work by random actions and observe their results: that is, by trial and error. "We had no theoretical information to guide so we had to proceed by trial and error." Polite.

Trouble and strife
Cockney rhyming slang – trouble and strife = wife. Not used a lot today except in jokes. As with many Cockney expressions when the meaning is clear only the first part of the expression is used. "I got home late last night and my trouble wanted to know where I'd been." Sexist and old-fashioned.

Truth of the matter
The essential fact of a situation. "You may have a GPS but we're out of range and he may have a map but he doesn't know where we are and we can't see any landmarks. The truth of the matter is we're lost." Polite.

Tuppence worth
Two pennies (tuppence) do not add up to much so this is a comment on a person's need to express his opinion. "Whenever there's a discussion he has to have his tuppence worth even though he knows nothing about the subject." Almost polite.

Turn a blind eye
Horatio Nelson was blind in one eye and when his admiral ordered him to withdraw at the Battle of Copenhagen (1801) he put his telescope to his blind eye and said, "I see no signal" and carried on to win the battle. The expression has changed its meaning so that today it would be the admiral who would turn a blind eye to his vice-admiral's indiscretion. "Her tutor turned a blind eye to her inability to arrive on time. This was nothing to do with her charm and good looks – just that she got top marks in all her papers." Polite.

Turned his toes up
He died – referring to the laid-out position of the corpse. It is a dispassionate and jocular statement. You would not say this about a recently deceased member of the family except, possibly, many years later when one is able to be detached. "It was 1981 when my father turned his toes up." Polite.

Twiddling thumbs

Clasping hands together and revolving one thumb over the other is a sign of boredom or lack of inspiration. In me it can be positive and indicative but in others it is a sign of incompetence and lack of drive. The expression is usually metaphorical. "I'm just sitting here twiddling my thumbs waiting to be told what to do." or "I wanted some sign of commitment from them but they just sat there twiddling their thumbs." Polite.

Two sandwiches short of a picnic

This phrase was popularised by John Major, Margaret Thatcher's successor as Prime Minister in the UK. It is a jocular way of saying that a person is mentally deficient or has not thought a problem through. "When it comes to his ideas on immigration, frankly he's two sandwiches short of a picnic." Polite.

U

Umpteen
Numbers after twelve go into the teens – thirteen, fourteen and so on up to nineteen. So "umpteen" is any large number. Frustrated mother to child "I've told you umpteen times you're not to play with the bread knife. You'll end up cutting yourself." Polite.

Under the belt
Getting something under the belt means achieving a goal before moving on – a bit like having a good meal before setting out on a long journey. "He needed first to pass his exams but once he'd got that under his belt he was intent on gaining practical experience." Polite.

Up and coming
This describes a young man or woman who shows signs of future prominence in their chosen field. "The

1997 General Election produced a group of up and coming young female MPs and the Prime Minister, Tony Blair, encouraged them. They became known as Blair's Babes." Polite.

Up and running
Getting machinery up and running means fully installing it and standing by to ensure nothing goes wrong. "His wife will not be pleased but he's not going on holiday until everything is up and running." Polite.

Up his street
When a person is knowledgeable on a subject or project and has lived with it at close quarters we say "It's right up his street" meaning that he has intimate and practical knowledge of it. "I was so glad he was appointed to chair the Health Commission as it is right up his street." Polite.

Up to the eyes
This is metaphorical, not physical. It means overloaded with work or debt. "The idea of going away for the weekend was appealing but he was up to his eyes in work and had to decline." Polite.

Upper crust
This is to do with skimmed milk not a loaf of bread. To make cream you let the warm milk settle and a crust forms of the richest part – the cream. So with society – the upper crust are the wealthy, old established families who are expected to set the tone for society as a whole. "You could sense from the cut of his suit and his good manners that he was upper

crust." Polite.

Upset the applecart

A costermonger's barrow is laden with fruit and vegetables. If you knock it over the vegetables spill but the apples will roll the furthest. So upsetting the applecart is causing distress and disrupting someone's plans. "Aunt Mary had organised a party for her niece but she upset the applecart by announcing that she had already booked to go to Milan that week with her boyfriend." Polite.

Use your loaf

Cockney rhyming slang: loaf of bread = head. So it means "Think about it" or use your initiative. "When you work for him you're expected to use your loaf." Polite.

W

Warts and all
Famously Oliver Cromwell is said to have told Sir Peter Lely, to paint his exact portrait without any flattery (in contrast to royalty who expected the opposite). His face had growths that appear in his death mask confirming that the artist did as he was asked. So the expression means "with no flattery or favourable misrepresentation." Polite.

Watching paint dry
Paint dries very slowly and you can't speed it up by watching it. So this is having to endure a boring or frustrating time e.g. sitting with a patient in a coma. "It's like watching paint dry." Polite.

Weasel words
Weasel words have more than one meaning. They appear on the surface to be acceptable but on closer

examination leave a let-out for the speaker who can interpret them differently later. "The Prime Minister's promise of a judge-led enquiry to look into the matter sounded good but these are weasel words because he gives no promise of action on the enquiry's findings." Polite.

Weather eye
Before the days of weather forecasts on radio and TV it was useful to acquire an understanding of the skies to anticipate what the weather was going to do. The meaning has carried over to apply to any uncertain situation. "It would be wise to keep a weather eye on the competition especially if they start reducing their prices." Polite.

Welly
Welly is short for wellington boot which is waterproof but clumsy, especially when driving a vehicle. So giving it welly is driving fast, ostensibly because your footwear is clumsy. "You'll have to give it a bit of welly or we'll be late." Polite.

Went to town
"Town" is a synonym for the big city so to go to town means to spend big money. "It wasn't their Silver Wedding but they went to town and invited everybody they could think of to their party." Polite.

When all's said and done
When there are points for and against there comes a time when a judgement has to be made. This is summing up before taking such a decision. "He has made a few mistakes but when all's said and done he

knows his subject and he's a good leader and I trust his judgement." Polite.

When the chips are down
This comes from roulette where, when the bets are placed, they cannot be removed. "With clothing you design the garment, lay out your capital in material and production and train the seamstresses. But when the chips are down it all depends on fashion and the public's whim whether the garments sell or not." Polite.

White lie
Sometimes it is judicious to be less than wholly truthful or to modify an adverse comment. This is a white lie - an acceptable lie on the borderline between tact and evasion. "He asked me if I'd enjoyed the play and, as he'd paid for the tickets, I told a white lie and said the acting had been good. Actually the whole thing was dire but he would have been so upset if I'd told him the truth." Polite.

Whitewash
In Cromwell's time (1640-50) pictures on church walls were considered to break the second commandment regarding graven images. Many churches covered them with whitewash (lime-based thin paint) rather than destroy them. By the same reasoning a report that exonerates significant people is said to be a whitewash. "The Chilcot Report into the Iraq war looks as though it's going to be a whitewash due to the American intervention in the publication of letters between Bush and Blair." Polite.

Whole shebang
There is no specific meaning for this word. It implies any rickety contraption or building that may well collapse under pressure. "He is very proud of his home-made car but he's no engineer: the whole shebang is unreliable and I would never go out in it!" Polite.

Wide berth
Give it a wide berth means keep well away from it. A shipping term originally, but can be applied to a person or situation that the speaker believes should be avoided. "I'd give it/him a wide berth if I were you." Polite.

Wide of the mark
A polite way of saying that the statement in question is not wholly true. "What he says is right as far as it goes but it is wide of the mark and needs some qualification." Polite.

Willy-nilly
This is a corruption of "Will I nill I" meaning whether I want to or not. "He was a witness to the accident so willy-nilly he was forced to give evidence in the case against his friend." Polite.

Wing and a prayer
In WWII there was a popular song about a shot-up plane that is brought back to base "coming in on a wing and a prayer". Applied more widely, it suggests that success is unlikely given the circumstances. "The project offers a lot but the budget is small so they are flying on a wing and a prayer." Polite.

With a vengeance
This means with great force or enthusiasm. "After a brief sunny spell the rain returned with a vengeance and we all got soaked." Polite.

Word in edgeways
To get a word in edgeways means to interrupt a speaker in mid-flow – not always easy to achieve! "She is a politician and talks incessantly. It is difficult to get a word in edgeways when she's speaking." Polite.

Work your socks off
Work extra hard. Mostly used in the past tense, not as an encouragement to do better. "He worked his socks off to get the job done by the weekend." Polite.

Works like a dream
When a new machine or an action plan provides the perfect solution to a process or problem it is said to work like a dream. Why a dream? Because dreams are usually beyond our expectations. "The new Sulzer machine was expensive but it works like a dream and has cut our process time by 40%." Polite.

World and his wife
Alliteration meaning too many people – a large crowd and not necessarily people you know or want to know. "We went down to Bognor for a quiet weekend but the world and his wife were there so we came home again." Polite.

Worse for wear
This has no reference to clothes wearing out but to

having drunk too much alcohol. It is a typical English understatement (Private Eye, the satirical magazine, coined the phrase "tired and emotional" to avoid libelling a politician renowned for bad moments.) "When I saw him after the party he was very much the worse for wear and definitely should not have been driving." Polite.

Write home about
Especially in WW1 soldiers would write home to tell their families that they were OK. Their letters were heavily censored as to what they could write so often there was nothing to write home about. This became an expression meaning not very important. "He may have run a half- marathon but so have many others and it's nothing to write home about." Polite.

Wrong side of the bed
Traditionally getting out of the wrong side of the bed puts you in a bad mood all day. "I should keep out of his way if I were you. He got out of the wrong side of the bed this morning and he's like a bear with a sore head." Polite but disrespectful.

ABOUT THE AUTHOR

Colin Grey left school at 16 to train as a Chartered Accountant. Finding the profession was not for him, he left immediately after qualifying for a career in industry. He spent 6 years in the oil industry with two major companies, including two years in Holland, followed by 5 years in Management Consultancy with a leading firm of practitioners which took him into many different industries before entering the City to oversee a wide variety of differing investments for a quoted Lloyd's insurance broker.

Subsequently he moved to a major Lloyd's reinsurance broker to manage their support and processing services. They transferred this operation (some 300 people) to Essex in 1992. He retired in 1994 after 40 years in the City and since then has travelled with his wife, Anne, extensively to many parts of the world.

He continues to retain an interest in promoting the understanding of English consequent on his experience in Holland and Ukraine. He maintains a regular correspondence with Olga Kuzina (see below) who lives in Sevastopol and is now Russian.

Please feel free to contact the author by email at colingrey365@gmail.com with any comments or queries you may have. We learn by others' experience: not least in the use of our own language.

ACKNOWLEDGMENTS

Many friends and family members have contributed to this book - some without knowing it - and I thank them all for their contributions. Since 2013 I have listened carefully to their conversation and noted on a pocket tape recorder phrases and expressions whose meaning or emphasis may not be immediately apparent.

We English delight in transporting ideas from one scenario to another. For example, "It isn't cricket" has nothing to do with the game. It simply means "It's not fair" or "It's not done" and can even be ironic. Similarly, if we say "He's for the high jump" this means he's in trouble and is going to be reprimanded. It has nothing to do with athletics!

I should like, in particular, to thank Olga Kuzina who was our tour guide on a cruise down the River Dnieper in 2013. Her English was so good and so full of idiom that we took her on one side to ask where she had learnt it. Her reply stunned us, "I've never been out of the country. But I do teach English at Sevastopol University." Lucky students! When we returned home I emailed Olga with a list of 20 phrases and the question, "How many of these would you use and be comfortable with in normal conversation?" Her answer was, "3 but would you please explain the other 17". These were the origin of this book.

My thanks are also due to Sally Jenkins for her professional help in designing and publishing this book. She offers a critique service for novice writers which has proved extremely helpful. Details can be found at http://sally-jenkins.com/first-impressions-critique-service.

Needless to say, this book would never have seen the light of day without the constant support and forbearance of Anne, my wife, who was in many ways its originator by noting down Olga's use of idiom.

All royalties from the sale of this book go to the Aidan Woodcock Charitable Trust which sponsors young professional musicians and helps them to develop their careers. Details of this charity and its work are available on www.maiastra.org.

If you found Speak the English the English Speak Volume 1 interesting or useful, please consider leaving a review on Amazon. This will help future readers decide whether or not to buy the book and thus support the charity.

Printed in Great Britain
by Amazon

33243547R00092